THE WEEK THAT CHANGED THE WORLD

ERNEST C. WILSON

NITY BOOKS • LEE'S SUMMIT, MO.

U NITY IS A link in the great educational movement inaugurated by Jesus Christ; our objective is to discern the truth in Christianity and prove it. The truth that we teach is not new, neither do we claim special revelations or discovery of new religious principles. Our purpose is to help and teach mankind to use and prove the eternal Truth taught by the Master.—*Charles Fillmore, founder of Unity*

CONTENTS

The Week That Changed the World

How It Began

IT IS given to only a few men to change the course of history. It was given to one man —Jesus Christ—to change the world. And of all the days of His short span of life, it was the last week, perhaps, that changed it most of all— the seven days (from His final entry into the city of Jerusalem) by which the die was cast.

A week that changed the world.

Five things done by Jesus especially roused the established authorities against Him, precipitating a decision on His part, and a cataclysmic succession of events by which Jesus wrested victory from defeat:

He cast out evil spirits from an afflicted man;

He dined with a Pharisee without conforming to the custom of washing before the meal;

He set aside the restrictions on what a Jew might eat;

He healed a sick woman on the sabbath, and finally,

He raised Lazarus from the dead!

It was this miracle that sealed His fate as far as the Jewish authorities were concerned.

"So the chief priests and the Pharisees gathered the council, and said, 'What are we to do? For this man performs many signs. If we let him go on thus, every one will believe in him, and the Romans will come and destroy both our holy place and our nation . . . So from that day on they took counsel how to put him to death. Jesus therefore no longer went about openly among the Jews, but went from there to the country near the wilderness, to a town called Ephraim; and there he stayed with the disciples."

It has been conjectured that Jesus went to Ephraim to escape the danger of death—which He was so soon to invite in Jerusalem. There is another very human, very understandable reason for His journey. Strong men are less likely to be seen going *from* something than *toward* something. It is a matter of motivation. Jesus was drawn "to the country near the wilderness" for a reason that reaches back to the beginning of His ministry.

At that time, when the very heavens opened and He saw God's spirit descending like a dove, and a voice out of heaven proclaiming, "This is my beloved Son, with whom I am well pleased," to Jesus humanly it must have seemed that all men would hear Him gladly, as indeed we are told the common people did. In His divine nature even then Jesus must have had intimations of challenge, if not from others at least from within Himself; for as we are told, almost immediately He went apart up onto a high mountain place where He faced the temptations of worldly power and acclaim—and rejected them.

How natural then that He should return to this same area, to Ephraim, a place apart, when the thoughts of human travail and of spiritual destiny together filled His mind and heart. "Now is my soul troubled. And what shall I say? 'Father, save me from this hour'? no, for this purpose I have come to this hour."

From this point on the tenor of His ministry changes. There is a greater intensity, a greater urgency in His message. His often playful manner of speech, the easy camaraderie with the twelve is gone. The inevitability of the way He is to go is in sharp focus. He is more withdrawn, more pensive.

As He "went about all the cities and villages, teaching in their synagogues . . . some Pharisees came, and said to him, 'Get away from here, for Herod wants to kill you.' And he said to them, 'Go and tell that fox, "Behold, I cast out demons and perform cures today and tomorrow, and the third day I finish my course. Nevertheless I must go on my way today and tomorrow and the day following; for it cannot be that a prophet should perish away from Jerusalem." '

" 'O Jerusalem, Jerusalem, killing the prophets and stoning those who are sent to you! How often would I have gathered your children together as a hen gathers her brood under her wings, and you would not!' "

Why was Jesus so persistent in proceeding toward Jerusalem? If He was to be slain it must be in Jerusalem, fulfilling prophecy. And it must be at the time of the Passover.

That last great tragedy could have been avoided. Jesus repeatedly had been warned not to enter Jerusalem. He had refused to accept that counsel.

The three years of His ministry had proved to Him that not even His closest companions had gained the true import of His ministry. To flee into obscurity now, before the threat of Rome, would be to lose whatever had been gained in those three years. It would mean oblivion for the revelation which was His own particular gift to the world. It would imply a defeat of the principle of love and nonresistance which had characterized His message.

He might return to Nazareth and resume His trade as a carpenter. Doubtless He could retain a certain following. Rome would not trouble Him. His enemies would be glad to be rid of Him so easily.

His message, however, would possibly never reach beyond the two kingdoms. He would be remembered as just another thwarted man of vision; another minor prophet, ground under the heel of materiality.

So far as Palestine went, His mission was a failure, but through His personal sacrifice He might yet gain the world for His Father.

All this must have been very clear to Jesus.

He made His decision. "From that time Jesus began to show his disciples that he must . . . suffer many things from the elders and chief priests and scribes, and be killed, and on the third day be raised."

He set His course. And thus began a week that changed the world.

Palm Sunday

"AND when they drew near to Jerusalem
and came to Bethphage, to the Mount of Olives,
then Jesus sent two disciples, saying to them,
'Go into the village opposite you, and immediately you will find an ass tied, and a colt with
her; untie them and bring them to me. If any
one says anything to you, you shall say, "The
Lord has need of them," and he will send them
immediately.' This took place to fulfill what
was spoken by the prophet, saying,
'Tell the daughter of Zion,
 Behold, your king is coming to you,

Humble, and mounted on an ass, and on a colt,
    the foal of an ass.'
Most of the crowd spread their garments on
the road, and others cut branches from the trees
and spread them on the road. And the crowds
that went before him and that followed him
shouted, Hosanna to the Son of David! Blessed
is he who comes in the name of the Lord!
Hosanna in the highest!"

John, describing the same scene, though
more briefly, was more specific. He tells us that
the crowd "took branches of palm trees and
went out to meet him," and "your king is coming, sitting on an ass's colt."

Jesus and His followers approached Jerusalem by way of Gilead, crossing the Jordan
westward to Ephraim where He rested before
going on to Jericho. There He healed blind
Bartimaeus, and dined with Zacchaeus, then
proceeded to Bethany, the home of Mary and
Martha, where Mary anointed His feet with the
precious oil. From Bethany He sent two of His
disciples to nearby Bethpage to secure the ass's
colt on which He was to ride into the holy city,
as if He knew the animal would be there when
needed, as indeed it was.

Again the long arm of prophecy reaches to
fulfillment. Had not Zechariah cried, "Rejoice
greatly, O daughter of Zion! . . . Lo, your king

comes to you; triumphant and victorious is he, humble and riding on an ass, on a colt the foal of an ass"?

If today you were to approach Jerusalem from the Trans-Jordan as did Jesus, you might be most conscious of the rocky, whitened character of the hills; sheep nibbling at the nearly invisible vegetation, perhaps a train of camels on the distant sky line. Between the hills of Judea and the mountains of Moab, and winding in the deep plain between, you would see a slender meandering streak of green—the willows, tamarisks, and shrubs that border the Jordan river on its way from the Sea of Galilee to the Dead Sea.

The plain is about fourteen miles wide at Jericho, once famous for its lavish groves of banana trees, date palms, balsam, fruit, and grain. Pilgrims journeying from Galilee to Jerusalem went by way of the mountain road to Jericho, thence over the rise of the Mount of Olives and across the Kidron Valley to the holy city.

How many times had Jesus stood upon the Mount and looked across at Jerusalem! As He approached it now what must His thoughts have been? Did He remember the time He came as a youth of twelve and talked with the wise men in the temple? The times between when He had

accompanied His father, come to pay their tax
to Rome, and watched the caravans on their way
between the East and West; or wandered
through the narrow streets, observing with ever-
heightened perception the people, Greeks, Romans, Jews, Bedouins; the wares in the shops
and markets, donkeys laden with produce, shepherds and goatherds guiding their charges
through the narrow ways; over all the chatter
of people's voices in a dozen tongues, the loud
cries of merchants hawking their wares?

Long ago—was it only three years ago?—
the picture of Himself as king of the world had
been presented to Him, and He had rejected it.
Today again He rejected it, but claimed a
greater sovereignty. Earthly rulers might appear
on mighty chargers, caparisoned alike in costly
raiment, with trumpeters going before.

Jesus chose the humblest of beasts, the ser-
vitor of the common people. Today He appeared in His spiritual nature as the Messiah.
Subtly He proclaimed His rejection of earthly
power. His kingdom—as He had asserted time
and again—was not of this world.

He stood where mortal man had stood, yet
He sat where never man had sat. Close as a
friend and neighbor, He was nevertheless mys-
teriously alone. He accepted the plaudits of the
crowd. "Rebuke your disciples," demanded

some of the Pharisees amongst them. And He answered, "I tell you, if these were silent, the very stones would immediately cry out." That they were not truly acclaiming Him as king of heaven but an earthly king—their earthly king —is implied by their swift falling away when He would not so proclaim Himself.

"Come with us—our way!" is the repeating cry of mortal man. "Come with me—God's way!" is the invitation of the Christ. We tell ourself it is hard to know the difference. It is often harder for us to yield the cherished longings of the mind and heart to a wisdom and a love much greater than our own. "Trust God," He is telling us in many ways. He entered Jerusalem not to fulfill His human will as Jesus, but His divine purpose as Christ. He did not even choose an animal that was trained and tractable, but the unbroken, wild, shaggy little creature— the colt. Who—except Himself perhaps—could know how it would react to being ridden, how it would act in crowds, and noisy crowds at that? But Jesus was never known to make choices on the basis of His own comfort and safety. It was not the first, nor would it be the last time that He would surprise the world (and the worldly) by the servants He had chosen— the shaggy, wild, untrained instruments of a purpose higher than they could understand.

His nature in us is today the same. It calls us to heights of daring. It seems at times to put all things at risk. It points to uncharted ways sometimes at variance with worldly security or acclaim. One of the surest ways that the uninitiated may learn to distinguish between His guidance and the prompting of his own self-seeking nature is that the latter will change with the shifting winds of expediency; His guidance, like its source, is without variableness, neither shadow that is cast by turning.

O Lord Christ, as I would receive the blessings and the promises of the kingdom, so I would also accept the discipline. After Your example, I will strive to ride and master the unbroken, unbridled side of my nature that can be compared to the colt on which You rode with such majesty and humility. In times of human favor and acclaim I will hold the rein on willfulness. Let my will and persistence claim higher goals than worldly gain alone. Like one who was to follow You, I would not be found unfaithful to the heavenly vision. I would keep the faith, run the course, follow the light, as Your inward nature grants me to see the light. In acceptance let me be humble, in rejection undismayed, in all things steadfast.

The Unfruitful Fig Tree

"AND ON the following day, when they came from Bethany, he was hungry. Seeing in the distance a fig tree in leaf, he went to see if he could find anything on it. When he came to it, he found nothing but leaves, for it was not the season for figs. And he said to it, 'May no one ever eat fruit from you again.'"

Jesus returned from Jerusalem each night with the Twelve and walked the four miles to the city each morning. Seeing a fig tree in leaf He had every reason to think that it would offer figs as well, unless others had stripped it of its fruit. When He found that it had borne no figs, He expressed disappointment.

For although it was not yet time for figs, yet having leaves the tree should also have borne figs, because of the peculiar characteristic of fig trees. A sign of spring in areas where the fig trees grow is the appearance on their bare branches of the tiny nubbins of figs. As the figs grow larger, leaves begin to appear, so that "consequently on a fig tree in full leaf one expected to find mature fruit; leaves without fruit indicated a sterile condition, a valueless tree. That the season was too early for normal fig production was apparently irrelevant; the first figs of the season were not usually ripe till May or June, and the cursing of the untimely fig tree occurred in April or even earlier," writes Alistair MacKay in his book "Gardening in the Bible."

This is almost surely an allegorical narrative, not intended to be taken literally. But it is a graphic illustration of a person who knows the Truth yet does not live it. "If you know these things, blessed are you if you do them," He said on another occasion.

Many of us are "overread and underdone." What we profess we must also seek to express. Or as Paul put it in his letter to the church at Rome, "Happy is he who has no reason to judge himself for what he approves."

"Of course I know better, but—" is an expression by which we excuse ourself for not living up to some form of truth we know.

J. R. Dummelow, in his "One-Volume Bible Commentary," says of this incident, in part: "The whole incident is an acted parable. There is no reason to suppose that Jesus was really hungry (He had no doubt had breakfast before starting out for Jerusalem that morning) or expected to find figs. . . . His words and actions were entirely symbolic, like those of the prophets."

He goes on to say: "The one fig tree, standing apart from all other trees, is the Jewish nation, and whereas it alone had leaves, while the other trees were bare, it signifies that whereas Israel made great professions of righteousness and of the service of God, the other nations of the earth made none. Both Jew and Gentile were, indeed, equally unfruitful, but the Jew added to his unfruitfulness the appearance of fruit, for it is a peculiarity of the fig tree that its fruit appears and is well-developed before there is any sign of leaves. . . . The curse of perpetual barrenness pronounced by Jesus upon the fig tree, i.e. upon Israel, has received a signal fulfillment. In the time of Christ Judaism was an active missionary religion, making thousands of converts in every province of the empire, and leaving religious thought far beyond its own borders. Now it enrolls no proselytes."

O Lord, let me be like a tree planted by the river of waters, that brings forth its fruit in due season. I would be a doer of the word, and not a hearer only. Let my entire being, body, mind, soul, and spirit, my thoughts and words and deeds show forth the evidence of the truth I know and love. I rejoice in every evidence of truth made manifest in my life, humble in what I have attained, pressing ever forward to the attainment of my high goal in Christ Jesus. In His name, Amen.

By What Authority?

"AND they came again to Jerusalem. And as he was walking in the temple, the chief priests and the scribes and the elders came to him, and they said to him, 'By what authority are you doing these things, or who gave you this authority to do them?'

"Jesus said to them, 'I will ask you a question; answer me, and I will tell you by what authority I do these things. Was the baptism of John from heaven or from men? Answer me.'

"And they argued with one another, 'If we say, "From heaven," he will say, "Why then did you not believe him?" But shall we say,

"From men?" '—they were afraid of the people, for all held that John was a real prophet. So they answered, 'We do not know.' And Jesus said to them, 'Neither will I tell you by what authority I do these things.' "

Both Matthew and Mark tell us that Jesus "taught them as one who had authority, and not as their scribes." Surely He had many claims to be an especial authority, as the embodiment of the Christ spirit, but surely too in His human nature there had been a preparation that made that divine embodiment possible. This was recognized by the centurion who had an afflicted servant. Jesus offered to come to his house and heal him. "Lord, I am not worthy to have you come under my roof," the officer responded; "but only say the word, and my servant will be healed. For I am a man under authority, with soldiers under me, and I say to one, 'Go,' and he goes, and to another, 'Come,' and he comes, and to my slave, 'Do this,' and he does it."

It often takes authority to recognize authority.

A young man, preparing for the ministry, and doubting his own eloquence in the pulpit, hit upon what he thought was a very clever idea. He would look up the greatest sermons of the greatest ministers, memorize and deliver them, and thereby be a great speaker. But results were disappointing. The grandiloquent words coming from his lips lacked the impact, the authority, of those from whose learning, dedication, experience, and conviction they had originated.

The authority or lack of it was not in the words but derived from the man back of them.

We know *about* many things; that is knowledge. We deeply *know* a few things; that is wisdom.

We seem to know best the things that come out of a deep inner conviction. We identify this with experience. Yet we cannot limit this knowing to consciously remembered experience. There are some forms of knowledge that we seem to have brought with us. We have not had to learn them in remembered life. Yet we know them beyond peradventure. We do not have to learn them, or if instruction is required, it is so minimal as to suggest that we are simply relearning something that we have well known somehow, somewhere, sometime.

This form of experience suggests to us that we have somehow, somewhere, earned the knowledge, perhaps in another life, another time. It comes forth now again to serve us in the present.

For Jesus to have been born as the very embodiment of the Christ surely suggests that back of His Christly incarnation there must have been vast preparation, vast dedication to the will and the work of His Father—who, as He reminded us, is our Father as well.

Certainly people of Jesus' own time considered this possibility. It is evidenced in the disciples' answer to Jesus' leading question, "Who do men say that the Son of man is?"

"And they said, 'Some say John the Baptist, others say Elijah, and others Jeremiah or one of the prophets.' He said to them, 'But who do you say that I am?'

"Simon Peter replied, 'You are the Christ, the Son of the living God.' "

Whether it be from past-life experiences, or from our own subconscious mind or from the universal subconscious, there well up within us all fragments of the universal wisdom which, somehow, we have prepared ourselves to receive.

God will use any channel that is open to Him.

O Lord Jesus, beloved Elder Brother, we see in You the outpictured pattern of what God intended us all to be. For though transiently and most obviously we are sons of earth, eternally we are sons of God and heaven. We seek to be open channels through which God's healing love, His enlightening wisdom, His unifying understanding may flow. So quicken us that we shall think and feel and speak and act not from mortal sense only, but with the authority of that nature in us which is most like You. Erase from our thought and heart all that would stain or inhibit the clear flow of Your inspiration. Let us walk steadfastly and faithfully the path of God's appointing, knowing that nothing can defeat His purpose in us. Amen.

The Leaven of the
Pharisees and Sadducees

"JESUS said to them, 'Take heed and beware of the leaven of the Pharisees and Sadducees.' "

"Then said Jesus to the crowds and to his
disciples, 'The scribes and the Pharisees sit on
Moses' seat; So practice and observe whatever
they tell you, but not what they do; for they
preach but do not practice. They bind heavy
burdens, hard to bear, and lay them on men's
shoulders; but they themselves will not move
them with their finger. They do all their deeds
to be seen by men; for they make their phylac-
teries broad and their fringes long, and they

love the place of honor at feasts and the best seats in the synagogues, and salutations in the marketplaces, and being called rabbi by men. But you are not to be called rabbi, for you have one teacher, and you are all brethren. And call no man your father on earth, for you have one Father, who is in heaven. Neither be called masters, for you have one master, the Christ. He who is greatest among you shall be your servant; whoever exalts himself will be humbled, and whoever humbles himself will be exalted.' "

That a man cannot successfully serve two masters is a concept that Jesus reiterated again and again in various ways. Once he has come into spiritual awareness he cannot successfully turn back to less perceptive ways of living and doing, any more than a chick that was hatched can return into the shell from which it has escaped. Or as Jesus put it, "No one who puts his hand to the plow and looks back is fit for the kingdom of God."

The Christ way is a new way of life. The Pharisees and Sadducees represent "qualities in human consciousness that oppose or resist the Christ and should be eliminated."

There is something very subtle about the matter of the leaven. It seems like a tiny thing, yet "a little leaven leavens the whole lump" (the words used here are Paul's). Even those who feel that they are very well grounded in Christ's teachings, and are endeavoring to "go the whole way" in following Him, are tempted to think, "Well, this little matter (or that) will make no difference."

It is as insidious as prevarication. The man who sticks to the truth as regards some matter in which he is involved will never need to fear contradicting himself. He may make a mistake, but it will be an honest one. The person who is not telling the truth is almost certain to contradict himself and in consequence will pile one falsehood upon another until there is no semblance of credibility remaining.

The little leaven has indeed leavened the whole lump.

Years ago a man wrote a book whose dominant theme was "What would Jesus do?" To read the book nowadays is something of a challenge to patience, and some of the incidents may seem contrived. Yet the challenge of the question is as fresh as today and tomorrow. It is a challenge to everyone who seeks to follow in what early Christians called the Way. Indeed any of us may be confused as to what Jesus would do in some of the matters that face us day by day; yet if we are trying to give honest answers, are following the Way according to the best light we have, we may be sure that more light will be given us.

Paul, having persecuted the early Christians, saw a great light. He was blinded by it. But his blindness was not the kind that grows into deepening darkness, but rather into increasing light—or at least increasing awareness of and adjustment to a light that he had not known before.

The Pharisees and Sadducees are still with us. They are concerned with appearances, with conformity, with the letter of the law. They do not know the spirit, do not recognize it when they see it, and having become aware of it finally, want to reject it as involving too many changes, too much conflict with the established order. They are like a young man who once appealed to the writer to tell him about Unity's concept of life. He was a good young man, healthy, vigorous, wholesome—and earthy. He pondered the matter for a while and finally said: "Well, I guess I'll wait till I'm older. I'm having too much fun the way I am, now!"

Perhaps there is a time for all things; and "nothing is so powerful as an idea whose time has come." When it comes for any one of us it will mean adjustments. It may involve confusion. We may feel that we are losing something, without for a time seeing clearly what we are gaining. But others have gone this upward way before us. It is not an unknown or uncharted way. Jesus pointed the way—and went it, to the extreme that it meant more to Him than life. Indeed He relinquished life for Life.

O Lord Christ, give me the humility to walk beside You along the upward way from sense to soul. Let me see not only the smallness of what by comparison with You I appear to be, but the greatness of what, seen in You, I am ultimately to embody.

Help me to see with the vision of Spirit, to discriminate between the true and false, the temporal and the eternal. Help me to see myself as I am in the light of my becoming, to be patient with myself in the steps of growth by which I shall attain; tolerant of others in following the light as it is given them to see, but with courage to be myself, to walk by the light that shines from within me—Your light, O Christ, I pray!

Tribute to Caesar?

"THEN the Pharisees went and took counsel how to entangle him in his talk. And they sent their disciples to him along with the Herodians, saying, 'Teacher, we know that you are true, and teach the way of God truthfully, and care for no man; for you do not regard the position of men. Tell us, then, what you think. Is it lawful to pay taxes to Cæsar, or not?'

"But Jesus, aware of their malice, said, 'Why put me to the test, you hypocrites? Show me the money for the tax.' And they brought him a coin. And Jesus said to them, 'Whose likeness and inscription is this?' They said, 'Cæsar's.'

Then he said to them, 'Render therefore to Cæsar the things that are Cæsar's, and to God the things that are God's.' When they heard it, they marvelled: and they left him and went away."

This incident is one of several that seem to have been quoted to show the efforts at entrapment on the part of the Pharisees—and Jesus' trenchant responses. How swiftly He reaches beyond the superficial to the basic elements involved! But beyond this there is a very practical challenge for us in this present day.

Does faith in God as the Great Healer mean rejection of human and mundane channels of help?

An elderly woman who was having obvious physical difficulties was persuaded by her grown sons and daughters to allow a young physician to examine her for treatment.

"There's one thing I want you to understand," she told him. "I know that only God can heal me."

"I know that, too," the doctor said. "All we can do is help a little."

May it not be a reasonable procedure to "go first direct to God," and "go next to man as God directs"?

If we are in financial difficulties, shall we close our eyes to the actualities, and expect worded prayers, however sincere and beautiful, however true to principle, to bring supply?

There are instances where this seems to have worked well, though on studying the background of results we may be able to trace a well-made and logical preparation for a good outcome. Generally we can agree that most of our prayers are answered *through* us rather than *for* us. Giving and receiving are parts of the law of bounty.

The successful farmer does not simply sit on a fence and pray for a bountiful harvest. He puts his prayer into action by tilling the soil, sowing the seed, doing everything that his intelligence and experience indicate will best cooperate with nature in producing a bountiful crop.

In a few words, the practical Christian does not do less than a non-believer in obedience to the laws of nature and of men, but more. The non-believer may believe that results are dependent upon himself and worldly wisdom only. The believer considers these elements as only part of his reliance.

When the Roman tax collector demanded tribute of Jesus and His disciples, and the disciples complained to Jesus that they had no money with which to pay, Jesus gave a very practical answer, often misconstrued. He said in so many words: "Catch a fish. You'll find the money in the fish's mouth." In other words: "Peter, you're a fisherman. Work at your trade. That will provide the revenue!"

We do not err in the wise and sensible use of human and mundane channels to help fill our needs or give us pleasure, but rather in looking to these only, and failing to see that the power that makes them possible is the real source of our good, and they are channels only.

This earth is the plane of experience. Through fleshly embodiment we have the opportunity of learning how much (and how little) we know of the practical use of the truth we know. For while this earth is far from ideal as an environment in which to find everything in agreement with our personal whims and desires, it is practically perfect as a place in which to learn and to grow. Every year, every day, every moment provides opportunities. I render, perforce, to Cæsar the things that are Cæsar's. No matter how spiritual I may claim to be, I must still conform to the law of gravity. I must pay taxes. I must work, and sleep, and eat, and care for the body in which for a time I dwell. But I must also live above these things, and it is in living above them that I render unto God the things that are God's: my thoughts, feelings, attitudes, devotions—my very self.

Lord Christ, I give thanks for the knowledge that man does not live by bread alone, but by every word that proceeds out of the mouth of God; that though to human sense and transiently we are sons of earth, eternally and spiritually we are sons of God and heaven. I give thanks for the bounties and blessings of this earthly plane of being, for the opportunities to learn and grow that dwelling here affords; but let me not be so enthralled by these temporal things that I shall lose sight of the bounties and blessings that it alone cannot give; for it is in the remembrance and observance of these that I render unto God the things that are God's. In these do I yield myself to Him, and discover and rest in the assurance that underneath are the everlasting arms. Amen.

The Great
Commandment

"AND one of the scribes came up and heard them disputing with one another, and seeing that he answered them well, asked him, 'Which commandment is the first of all?'

"Jesus answered, 'The first is, "Hear, O Israel: The Lord our God, the Lord is one; and you shall love the Lord your God with all your heart, and with all your soul, and with all your mind, and with all your strength." The second is this, "You shall love your neighbor as yourself." There is no other commandment greater than these.'

"And the scribe said to him, 'You are right,

Teacher; you have truly said that he is one, and there is no other but he; and to love him with all the heart, and with all the understanding, and with all the strength, and to love one's neighbor as oneself, is much more than all whole burnt offerings and sacrifices.'

"And when Jesus saw that he answered wisely, he said to him, 'You are not far from the kingdom of God.' And after that no one dared to ask him any question."

If in giving our unstinted love to God we fear we shall be losing something, it is because we do not know God as Jesus did.

Jesus offered us no definition of God, but He revealed the nature of God by the way He lived, by the tenor of His thoughts and feelings, His words and actions. Jesus profoundly changed mankind's thinking about God. His is a joyous faith. Its spirit permeates the Gospels. A man may lose everything the world has to offer, and yet be rich if his faith is placed above them. The incident comes to mind of how an associate of Thomas Edison awakened the great inventor in the middle of the night to shout into his deafened ears that his factories, product of a lifetime's dedicated effort, were burning down.

"Go back to bed," Edison is quoted as saying. "We'll build some new ones tomorrow!"

A person may be dismayed by a financial loss, but if he has mental resources by which to replace his loss he is not overwhelmed. "Beware," said Jesus, in effect, "how you put your trust in earthly fortunes, for where your treasure is there will your heart be also."

He tells of a tenant farmer who accidentally came upon a treasure hidden in a field, and turned it up on the point of his plow. Palestine was like some of the central European countries which were often dominated by foreigners. In such a land, when the alien army marched through, or even a maurauding caravan of bandits, the safest place for a man's treasure to be was buried in the ground, with the hope that he would find it again later. Sometimes he did. Sometimes he forgot. Sometimes he died before passing on the secret.

So someone else, our treasure finder, comes upon it. Hastily he drops to the ground, casting his gaze about to be sure he is unobserved. His eyes sparkle with delight at the find. Sighting for landmarks, he hastily presses the treasure back into the earth out of sight. But from then on he can have no peace until somehow he has raised the money to buy the field and make the treasure uncontestably his own. Meantime he can think of nothing else. He cannot eat. He cannot sleep. He rises from his bed, makes his

way, skulking, to the field by night, thrusts his
hand into the loosened soil, his heart thumping,
as he gropes and finds the spot; feels the cool
surface of the box or jar that holds the treasure,
sighs and returns again to the house. Truly,
where a man's treasure is, there will his heart be
also!

"Seek first his kingdom and his righteousness, and all these things shall be yours as well"
was Jesus' promise. It does not always seem so,
and fearful man too often seeks what Jesus
called the added things first of all.

"What will it profit a man, if he gains the
whole world and forfeits his life?" "My life
can wait!" doubting man replies, and thereby
shuts the door against the greater good he might
have had.

As the whole is greater than any of its parts,
so is the love of God greater than the parts we
see separately—separately from God and from
one another: our love of beauty, our love of
vital health, our love of life itself. Oneness with
the source of these is more desirable than oneness with any one or all of them. All are, or well
may be, good, but He is goodness itself, the
all-enfolding, all-encircling Good.

Lord Christ, I would not be so enthralled
by the earthly beauties and blessings of my life
that I lose sight of their source. Let me hold all

things with appreciation but none so tightly that their loss seems overwhelming. Let my faith be so God-centered that it includes but is above possessions. My faith is stayed on Thee. Amen.

How Much Shall
I Give?

"AND he sat down opposite the treasury,
and watched the multitude putting money into
the treasury. Many rich people put in large
sums. And a poor widow came and put in two
copper coins, which make a penny.

"And he called his disciples to him, and
said to them, 'Truly, I say to you, this poor
widow has put in more than all those who are
contributing to the treasury. For they all con-
tributed out of their abundance; but she out
of her poverty has put in everything she had,
her whole living.' "

"One man gives freely, yet grows all the

richer; another withholds what he should give, and only suffers want," said Solomon. Everyone who seeks to apply Truth principles to his daily living soon discovers the truth that giving and receiving are the dual aspects of prosperity and well-being. As we give, so shall we receive; and the giving comes first. Even in prayer, we can get a clear response only as we give our whole attention to a listening attitude of mind and heart. In a service we render, in a vocation in which we desire to be proficient, half measures are not enough. The person who gives less than his best, less than that of which he is capable, cheats himself.

With all our giving we can never give as much as God gives to us; but one of the ways of trying is in *thanks*giving; giving not in expectation of return, whether our giving be thanks-giving or the rendering of a service, or concentrated attention to a subject, or disbursing funds (though the return is inevitable under the law of equilibrium or balance) but because it is Godlike to give: because we rise into a recognition of our true nature as sons of God when we live in what in the parlance of the day is called involvement.

The widow, giving her two mites, was not thinking of a return. She was trying with all her heart to express her thanks for what God

had given to her. And her giving drew Jesus'
pointed comment because of this.

We make many laws for ourself that are not
God-made. We think of our supply as limited to
what we manifestly possess, supply that is ex-
hausted by use. We look to a return on a basis
of trading or bartering, which is not truly giving
at all. We expect appreciation and compensa-
tion directly from those to whom in manner we
have given ("I've worked my fingers to the
bone for him and he doesn't appreciate it"),
whereas under God's law our bounty and supply, our recognition and response often come
from unexpected quarters.

*I give as I would receive, richly, freely,
promptly, generously, in the Father's name and
spirit. I give because it is Godlike to give. I give
because I have received so much from life. I
give because I am able to give, because I want to
give, because it makes me feel good to give. I
put a blessing upon every service I render, upon
the ideas I share with others, the appreciation
and opinions I express, the checks I write, the
currency I dispense, so that others may feel the
joy and happiness I find in giving, sharing,
communicating. I praise God that He permits
me to be a channel of service, of bounty, of well-
being, of creative ideas. I give and receive in
His name and spirit.*

The Divine Paradox

"Now among those who went up to worship at the feast were some Greeks. So these same came to Philip, who was from Bethsaida in Galilee, and said to him, 'Sir, we wish to see Jesus.' Philip went and told Andrew; Andrew went with Philip and they told Jesus.

"And Jesus answered them, 'The hour has come for the Son of man to be glorified. Truly, truly, I say to you, unless a grain of wheat falls alone into the earth and dies, it remains alone; but if it dies, it bears much fruit.

" 'He who loves his life loses it, and he who

hates his life in this world will keep it for eternal life.' "

Luke renders the thought of this last statement a little more clearly when he says, "Whoever would save his life will lose it: and whoever loses life for my sake, he will save it."

To be most creative, most productive in life, indeed we do have to lose our life—lose ourself—in whatever we are doing; to be so intent on the matter in hand that we forget to question whether it will be profitable, whether it is worth the trouble, whether we are running overtime, or are missing a meal, or getting tired. For the sake of the creative, inspiring higher nature within us, the Christ nature, we become committed to the task. We love our life, yet by the same token we find ourself in a most marvelous and rewarding way. For no weariness, or hunger, or privation, no bruises to the human body matter when we are dedicated to some project, whether it is digging a ditch or building a skyscraper or carving a statue out of marble or carving a book out of words. We "lose ourself," or more actually, we lose our sense of bondage to things, circumstances, obligations, and acting as a free spirit, we let that spirit soar, and feel the Shekinah glory descend upon us, rise up within us.

O, fill me with Your spirit, Lord, that I may

walk and work and live in the consciousness of Your holy presence. Let me be so imbued with that awareness that I behold that presence in everyone I contact, in all the elements of the world about me. Let me so uplift the daily task that I too am uplifted, and that others, beholding, respond at unawares. Truly, if You be lifted up in me, all will be drawn to You, seeing not me, but You in me.

Jesus Foretells Changes

"JESUS left the temple and was going away, when his disciples came to point out to him the buildings of the temple. And Jesus answered them, 'You see all these, do you not? Truly, I say to you, there will not be left one stone upon another, that will not be thrown down.'

"As he sat on the Mount of Olives, the disciples came unto him privately, saying, 'Tell us, when will this be, and what will be the sign of your coming and of the close of the age?'

"And Jesus answered, 'Take heed that no man leads you astray. For many will come in my name, saying, "I am Christ," and they will lead many astray. And you will hear of wars

and rumors of wars; see that you are not
alarmed; for this must take place, but the end
is not yet. For nation will rise against nation,
and kingdom against kingdom, and there will
be famines and earthquakes in various places:
all this is but the beginning of the suffering.

" 'Then they will deliver you up to tribulation, and put you to death; and you will be
hated by all nations for my name's sake. And
then many will fall away, and betray one another, and hate one another. And many false
prophets will arise, and lead many astray. And
because wickedness is multiplied, most men's
love will grow cold. But he who endures to the
end will be saved.' "

People tend to interpret Bible prophecies
in terms of their own lifetime, and with personalities in contemporary history. Thus the
prophecies of Jesus quoted above have been related to World War I, World War II, and the
so-called "little wars" of the present. Commentators generally consider the destruction of Jerusalem by Titus, A.D. 70, as the fulfillment of
Jesus' words.

Some of the fundamentalist cults relate the
prophecies of Daniel, Jesus, and John (in Revelation) to the nations of the world, i.e., the
bear as representing Russia, the eagle representing the United States, the bull representing

Great Britain. The "number of the beast" described in Rev. 13:18 has been related to various Popes of the Roman Catholic church, to former Kaiser Wilhelm of Germany, and later, to Hitler. Actually it appears to be derived from a system of numerical symbolism characteristic of the so-falled Lesser Mysteries of ancient Greek culture, in which 666 is the symbol of the lower or phrenic mind, as contrasted with 888, the higher mind in mankind.

Generally, the Bible may be taken as the spiritual history of mankind (his-story) in his journey from sense to soul, or in the terms of the New Testament, from the Cross to the crown of attainment. Along the way man comes through many wars, many storms and quakings. The story of Elijah, disputing with Jezebel, is a graphic illustration of this. Following his dramatic denunciation of her wrongdoings, he made his way to Mount Sinai. He experienced earthquakes, rainstorms, thunder and lightning, as he sought for guidance from on high. But he could not hear God's voice in them. It was only after the storms subsided that he heard "a still small voice." The significance here seems very plain: actually the storms were in Elijah, representative of the mental and emotional stress through which he was coming into a higher understanding.

No doubt at least in part, Jesus' prophecies about "the last days," the wars and rumors of wars, famines, pestilences, and so on, have to do with the efforts by which we all come out of old ways of thought and feeling into higher ones. Even "the last days" of His earthly ministry have a parallel in our individual growth and overcoming. "But he who endures to the end will be saved."

Grant me, O Lord, deep peace of mind, high courage, steadfast faith, as I journey on the upward path of spiritual attainment. I would be true to the truth I know, beholding in You what in truth I am, and what in fact I am to be. Help me to remember that one way in which I can help to overcome the wars and pestilences of the world about me is to withstand and displace them within me. "Let there be peace on earth, and let it begin with me."

The Betrayer

"NOW the feast of Unleavened Bread drew nigh, which is called the Passover. And the chief priests and the scribes were seeking how to put him to death, for they feared the people. Then Satan entered into Judas called Iscariot, who was of the number of the twelve; he went away and conferred with the chief priests and captains how he might betray him to them. And they were glad, and engaged to give him money. So he agreed, and sought an opportunity to betray him to them in the absence of the multitude."

Who shall be the greatest and who shall be

least in Christ's kingdom was a question that often troubled the Twelve. They did not understand what was meant by greatest, or least, or the kingdom itself. In many ways Jesus had tried to make them understand. On one occasion He called a little child to Him, and set him before them, and told them that they must become as little children, humble (and teachable?) to enter into His kingdom. He described it as a serious offense to mislead one of these who believed in Him.

Temptations must come, He granted, "but woe to the man by whom the temptation come!"

It seems a far cry from that incident to the assemblage at the last supper, and the sad words of Jesus, "The Son of man goes as it is written of him, but woe to that man by whom the Son of man is betrayed!"

Meantime the antagonism of the chief priests and scribes had crystallized into a definite plot to destroy Him. "For they feared the people," feared most of all that the mounting fame of Jesus would turn them against the "establishment" and toward Him. They found a ready instrument at hand. It was Judas.

"One of you is a devil," Jesus said, speaking to the Twelve: and at the Last Supper He made it plain that He was referring to Judas. The devil that tempted Judas was one that tempts

most all of us at one time or another, the devil
of self-interest. It was becoming clear that by
Jesus' own admission, even by His decision, His
doom was sealed. He had indicated that only
by His death would His kingdom be established.
To a calculating mind, such as Judas evidently
possessed, this negated Jesus' claim to Messiah-
ship, for the Jewish belief was that their Messiah
should not die, but live forever. Better then for
himself—even for Jesus, Judas may have rea-
soned—that he betray Him to the Jewish authorities, perhaps to the Sanhedrin. This should
at worst mean His banishment and excommuni-
cation, for the Jewish authorities did not have
the power of execution. Maybe too if things got
out of hand and the power of Rome was invoked, Jesus would at last use His seemingly
magical powers, and with a wave of His hand,
dispel or even slay His persecutors. For Judas,
who did not want to die, could not conceive
that Jesus really meant what He said about dying.

And if He should be slain, what of the disciples? What of himself, Judas of Kerioth?
"Guilt by association" did not begin with the
twentieth century.

The instinct of self-preservation is very
strong, strong enough to make most of us on
occasion justify a course of action that we might

not condone in somebody else. As Judas betrayed Christ, have we not sometimes betrayed the Christ nature in ourself? We suffer as a result, not because God demands it of us, but because we demand it of ourself. We suffer most when, at least theoretically, we "know better." Judas had been chosen of Jesus, He had lived with, walked with Jesus and the other apostles for three years. "He should have known better" than to doubt the wisdom and judgment of the Master. That he did not, seemingly could not, is the tragedy of Judas and of all of us who betray our own higher nature.

> *O Christ, Thou Son of God,*
> *My own eternal self;*
> *Live Thou Thy life in me,*
> *Do Thou Thy will in me,*
> *Be Thou made flesh in me.*
> *I will have no will but Thine,*
> *I will have no self but Thee.*
> —The Gaelic Prayer

The Passover

"THEN came the day of Unleavened Bread, on which the passover lamb had to be sacrificed. So Jesus sent Peter and John, saying, 'Go and prepare the passover for us, that we may eat it.' They said to him, 'Where will you have us prepare it?' He said to them, 'Behold, when you have entered the city, a man carrying a jar of water will meet you; follow him into the house which he enters, and tell the householder, "The Teacher says to you, 'Where is the guest-room where I am to eat the passover with my disciples?' " And he shall show you a large up-

per room furnished; there make ready.' And
they went, and found it as he had told them;
and they prepared the passover.''

The passover is an annual feast of the Jews,
instituted to commemorate the sparing the He-
brews in Egypt when ''the Lord smote all the
first-born in the land of Egypt.'' The feast con-
tinues for eight days. A feature of it is the
paschal lamb.

Jesus sent His two favorite disciples, Peter
and John, to prepare the Passover, and when
they asked Him where they should do this He
indicated that everything was arranged for.
They were to follow a man carrying a pitcher
of water and thereby be led to a lodging house
where they could abide during their stay in the
city. As George Lamsa tells us in his book
''Gospel Light,'' ''Families are often reluctant
to open their homes to single men because men
and women, guests and strangers all sleep in
the same room.''

There are two important applications to our
own life that can be gleaned from this experience.

The term *passover* comes down to us with
many meanings. It has been applied to the
Exodus—that is, to Moses' leading the children
of Israel out of Egypt, through the wilderness
(the passover) into the Promised Land. In early

American history, pioneers came to call any unfriendly or forbidding area that they must cross a "passover." In metaphysics the term can well describe the transitional state in which we are passing over from one state of consciousness, one level of awareness, to another; and in that connection the assurance Jesus gave the disciples that everything was prepared for them, and that they need only act on faith, was very timely and reassuring. "God is in the tares as well as in the wheat." He is with us in what seem adverse experiences as well as in those that appear favorable; and sometimes we find that we learn the most and are most greatly blessed through the ones that most challenge our faith and daring. A sense of this came to the Psalmist when he sang, "Thou preparest a table before me in the presence of my enemies."

When John the Baptist, preaching repentance by the waters of Jordan, saw his cousin Jesus approaching at the beginning of His ministry and cried, "Behold, the Lamb of God!" he was subtly implying that as the paschal lamb was a symbol of the passover from a state of bondage in Egypt to an anticipated state of freedom in the Promised Land of Canaan, so Jesus was the Lamb that should symbolize their passing from a state of bondage to material powers into a higher state of consciousness.

It was on Thursday morning of what we now call Holy Week that Jesus and His companions left Bethany for Jerusalem. Assyrian Christians observe the Jewish feast of the Passover on Thursday and the resurrection of Christ on the following Sunday. The place of meeting for Jesus and the disciples was provided without charge; the meat, bread, and other supplies were bought from the proprietor of the inn. But here again, Jesus is not only conforming to ancient Jewish custom, but is symbolically enacting the drama in which He Himself is to be the paschal lamb, offered as a sacrifice.

Seen from "the under side" (the human side of pain and suffering), this is a sad and seemingly needless ordeal, referred to in traditional Christianity as "the vicarious atonement" for the sins of humanity. Seen from the "upper side" of spiritual insight, it is Jesus' enactment of at-one-ment with all mankind, as described in John 17:21: "that they may all be one; even as thou, Father, art in me, and I in thee, that they also may be in us, so that the world may believe that thou hast sent me."

Now I see more clearly what You have been trying to tell men by Your words, and by Your word made flesh and called forth into supremely loving action—that God and I are one even as You and He are one; that You have prepared a passover for me, too; that I am to grow in wisdom and spiritual stature; that I am to experience a passover, and that the way is prepared in advance of my human need; that I need not fear the challenges of growth and change; that all has been provided for, and always will be. So I am strong in You, Lord; strengthened by Your spirit in the inward man, I shall walk in faith as You have given me to see that many —most of all, You, O Christ Jesus—have walked before me. Amen.

The Holy Communion

"AND when the hour came, he sat at table, and the apostles with him. And he said to them, 'I have earnestly desired to eat this passover with you before I suffer; for I tell you I shall not eat it until it is fulfilled in the kingdom of God.' And he took a cup, and when he had given thanks he said, 'Take this, and divide it among yourselves; for I tell you that from now on I shall not drink of the fruit of the vine until the kingdom of God comes.' And he took bread, and when he had given thanks he broke it and gave it to them, saying, 'This is my body.' "

Christian observance of the Lord's Supper is based upon Jesus' observance of the passover with the disciples. There is a belief in certain of the established churches that in the observance of the holy communion, or Eucharist, when the bread and wine are consecrated, they actually become the body and blood of Jesus Christ, only the *appearance* of bread and wine remaining. That millions of devout Christians could so celebrate the Lord's Supper must surely mean that they do it on blind faith, not thinking, or else that they have thought and prayed so deeply as to have discerned in this concept a profoundly mystical and symbolical experience. None of these persons, we should imagine, would willingly imbibe the flesh and blood of any ordinary human being, let alone that of Jesus Christ.

This observance, however, can be a reminder of the saving grace of the Master's life and love; and also of one of the great natural miracles of life, by which the food that we eat and the liquids that we drink become in effect our flesh and blood. That this may not have occurred to us as being at least as mysterious as the doctrine of transubstantiation is only because it is so commonly experienced that we simply accept it as a fact of life.

How, then, can what we eat and drink become the flesh and blood of Christ?

If we follow the admonition of Jesus to eat
and drink in remembrance of Him, and if our
spirit becomes so quickened that He comes to
dwell in us, as Paul assured us He would, then
truly what we eat and drink become, in our
bodies, mystically, the flesh and blood of Christ.

We must remember that in the time of
Jesus there was no Christian church as we now
know it, no Holy Eucharist, no robed priests
and censers, no forms and litanies. Might not
the simple Jesus, whose church was the hillside,
whose stained-glass windows were the over-
arching skies with their changing hues from
sunrise to darkness, feel out of place and strange
among some of the rites that have evolved out
of His life and teachings?

Did He, in His nature as the Messiah, actually intend that this last simple meal with
the Twelve who had become His close com-
rades through the three-year ministry should be
made the basis for a ritual considered essential
to salvation? It is possible. Certainly it has been
so accepted by countless people since He dwelt
among us so long ago.

But in His divinely human nature may He
not simply have been saying something like
this: "Beloved, I shall not be with you again
in quite the same way as we are together now,

but whenever you eat and drink to your body's nourishment, remember me, and my spirit will be with you. My love and wisdom will guide you in the trying days that are before you. Be of good courage. Be not afraid. As strength and energy fill your limbs from food and drink, so shall courage and faith enter into you from my nature within you. My flesh and blood— and most of all, my spirit—shall be formed in you."

"The Holy Supper is kept indeed,

In whatso we share with another's need."

Lord Christ, I acknowledge You as the truth of my eternal nature. I dedicate myself to the expression of Your nature in me. As through the nature of Jesus You have said that You had meat to eat that others knew not of, so do I now realize that I too have nourishment that is not of bread and wine alone, but of Your indwelling presence that vivifies, renews, vitalizes, and restores me. Not only when I imbibe food for my physical body, but when I respond to life and love and beauty, patience, and work and challenge, I feel attunement to Your all-pervading presence. Amen.

If You Know
These Things

"JESUS, knowing that the Father had given all things into his hands, and that he had come from God and was going to God, rose from supper, laid aside his garments, and girded himself with a towel. Then he poured water into a basin, and began to wash the disciples' feet, and to wipe them with the towel with which he was girded.

"He came to Simon Peter; and Peter said to him, 'Lord, do you wash my feet?' Jesus answered him, 'What I am doing you do not know now, but afterward you shall understand.' Peter said to him, 'You shall never wash my feet.' Jesus answered him, 'If do not I wash you, you have no part in me.' Simon Peter said to him, 'Lord, not my feet only, but also my hands and my head!' Jesus said to him, 'He who has bathed does not need to wash, except for his feet, but he is clean all over; and you are clean, but not all of you.' For he knew who was to betray him; that was why he said, 'You are not all clean.'

"When he had washed their feet, and taken his garments, and resumed his place, he said to them, 'Do you know what I have done to you? You call me Teacher and Lord; and you are right, for so I am. If I then, your Lord and Teacher, have washed your feet, you also ought to wash one another's feet. For I have given you an example, that you also should do as I have done to you. Truly, truly, I say to you, a servant is not greater than His master; nor is he who is sent greater than he who sent him. If you know these things, blessed are you if you do them.

" 'I am not speaking of you all; I know whom I have chosen: it is that the scripture may be fulfilled, "He who ate bread has lifted his heel against me." I tell you this now, before it takes place, that when it does take place you may believe that I am he. Truly, truly, I say to you, he who receives anyone whom I send receives me; and he who receives me receives him who sent me.' "

It would be most unusual nowadays for a host to greet a guest with the invitation, "May I wash your feet?" (Although it might not be unusual for him to ask, "Would you like to take a shower and freshen up after your journey?") Luxurious bathrooms, abundant hot water at the turn of a faucet are common today, at least in the Western world. So are paved highways, and automobiles, and airplanes.

In Jesus' day, and in the area where He spent His young manhood, there were few paved roads. They were dusty or muddy as the case might be. They were used alike by slow-moving animals pulling crude vehicles, or bearing riders, as well as by pedestrians. The sun can be hot in Palestine, and feet become weary and begrimed with only the scanty covering of sandals. What more natural, as a common courtesy, than to offer a basin of water, a towel, and the added grace of personal ministration? Jesus made of it a gesture of loving humility, a ceremonial prelude to the breaking of bread together.

A modern Unity couple have made a household byword of a familiar advertising catch phrase, "LSMFT." They interpret it, "Loving service, my first thought." There had been discussion among the disciples as to who would be greatest in the kingdom, and Jesus made it clear that the greatest is he who serves the best.

Peter protests that Jesus should not wash his feet, and Jesus implies the spiritual meaning of being washed, by declaring that "If I do not wash you, you have no part with me": that being washed meant the cleansing of the human nature. So Peter, always the extrovert, cries, "Lord, not my feet only but also my hands and my head!" In effect, Jesus says that if you are inwardly clean you do not need another baptism (of the head and hands), but that not all those assembled are thus clean, referring to Judas and his imminent betrayal of the Master.

His discourse following His washing of their feet makes it clear that this is an example; that as He has served them, so should they serve one another, to be doers of the word and not hearers only.

Here is one of the most challenging admonitions in Christian living: *"If you know these things, blessed are you if you do them."*

Emerson was to phrase it, "If you have light you must bear witness to the light." A famous preacher (Daniel Poling) tells about how his young man son once asked for an appointment with him in his study—an indication that the youth considered the proposed meeting of special import. "Dad, how much do you really know about God?" he challenged. Wisely, the father answered: "Well, not very much, son. But what I do know makes a lot of difference!"

What we do know about Christ and God may often seem to us to be very little compared to all that there must be to know. What is individually important to us is the use we make of what we know. When we think of the outstanding service that some persons have given to the world, or great overcomings of illness or poverty or other handicaps, we find that "God shows no partiality"; that these "doers" are not always the most erudite or wealthiest or most physically attractive, but often persons of lowly background, members of minority races or faiths, even victims of some handicap, who yet have come through "great tribulation" as the Master describes it.

Dear Father-God, help me to be faithful to the truth I know, and let my knowledge increase according to my faith. With Thy dear Christ I would be an overcomer, a doer of His word and not a hearer only. Let me be a channel of blessing to those around me, serving as I should like to be served, loving as I should like to be loved, understanding as I should like to be understood—doing the best I know, and leaving results to Thee.

Where the Devil Comes From

"ONE of his disciples, whom Jesus loved, was lying close to the breast of Jesus. Simon Peter beckoned to him and said, 'Tell us who it is of whom he spoke.' So lying thus, close to the breast of Jesus, he said to him, 'Lord, who is it?' Jesus answered, 'It is he to whom I shall give this morsel when I have dipped it.'

"So when he had dipped the morsel, he gave it to Judas, the son of Simon Iscariot. Then after the morsel, Satan entered into him. Jesus said to him, 'What you are going to do, do quickly.'

"Now no one at the table knew why he said this to him. Some thought that, because Judas had the money box, Jesus was telling him, 'Buy what we need for the feast'; or, that he should give something to the poor.

"So, after receiving the morsel, he immediately went out; and it was night."

"Satan entered into him," says John of Judas. A belief of olden times that still finds credence among certain sects of the present day is that many of men's misdeeds are not essentially of their own doing, but that an outside entity, a discarnate (and evil) personality has gotten into them and given them a compulsion to commit evil deeds. And the evildoer will disclaim his deed by asserting that "something" came over him, an irresistible force or impulse.

This concept seems to arise out of men's desire to reject what they instinctively know to be unworthy of them. Perhaps if Judas had been able to believe this he would not have felt the need to expiate his guilt by suicide.

A modern thinker would find difficulty in accepting the notion that "Satan entered into" Judas a moment after he had received the sop from Jesus, or that an evil spirit suddenly enters, as from an outside source, anyone's nature in the commission of crimes against self and others.

Job expresses what may be considered a very modern concept when he says (twice) that "the Lord said to Satan, 'Whence have you come?' Satan answered the Lord, 'From going to and fro on the earth, and from walking up and down on it.'"

There is nothing wrong about the earth as such, but man is not essentially an earthly creature—only transiently so. Eternally he is a son of God and heaven. But the earth and the things of earth can seem very powerful, very real to us if we allow ourself to become involved with them, very real and very insistent in their demands, and heaven can seem very vague and far away. This is what is meant by going to and fro "on" the earth, and up and down "on" it. So that the words in Job can very well mean not that the devil *returns* from going to and fro, up and down: but that the devil *results* from this.

We do not become an angel or a devil in a moment. It takes a long time for a man to become either one. It takes many deviations from a developed moral nature to finally give way to undisciplined transgressions. Often it begins with the apology, "Well, just this once won't matter," or, "Of course I know better, but—." By the same token it takes a great many efforts to embody the ideal of what we conceive to be

God's vision for us. For as the poet put it,
"Heaven is not reached at a single bound;
 But we build the ladder by which we rise
 From the lowly earth to the vaulted skies,
 And we mount to its summit, round by round."

The story is told of an artist who encoun-
tered a young man of such beauty of countenance
that he persuaded the youth to sit for him as a
model to represent Jesus. The artist determined
to paint a portrayal of each of the disciples. He
searched for years until he found someone
whose mien represented to him what Judas
would look like. The man he finally found
proved to be the same one who had posed for
the portrait of Jesus years before. He had come
to such a state, perhaps, from "going to and
fro on the earth, and . . . up and down on it."

*Let me be in the world but not overcome by
it, grateful for its blessings and opportunities,
yet not engulfed by them. Let not my many
possessions possess me; let me measure their
value only by their beauty and their usefulness.
Let me love all things good, yet none too much;
people too, not to possess but to bless and to be
blessed.*

Our Hope of Glory

"WHEN he had gone out, Jesus said, 'Now is the Son of man glorified, and in him God is glorified; if God is glorified in him, God will also glorify him in himself, and glorify him at once. Little children, yet a little while I am with you. You will seek me; and as I said to the Jews, so now I say to you, "Where I am going you cannot come." A new commandment I give to you, that you love one another; even as I have loved you, that you also love one another. By this all men will know that you are my disciples, if you have love one for another.'

"Simon Peter said to him, 'Lord, where are

you going?' Jesus answered, 'Where I am going you cannot follow me now: but you shall follow afterward.' Peter said to him, 'Lord, why cannot I follow you now? I will lay down my life for you.' Jesus answered, 'Will you lay down your life for me? Truly, truly, I say to you, the cock will not crow, till you have denied me three times.' "

The Phillips translation makes the first portion of this passage a little clearer: "Now comes the glory of the Son of man, and the glory of God in him. If God is glorified through him, then God will glorify the son of man—and that without delay." Jesus here is referring to His approaching travail, brought a step nearer by Judas' having left to arrange for His arrest. He repeats, as if to emphasize the very heart of His message, what the world needs today quite as much as (if not more than) in His own time— that those who follow Him are to love one another as He has loved the disciples. By this shall they (and we) be known as followers of the Way.

He speaks of going, in the resurrection, where the others cannot at least immediately follow.

"Why cannot I follow you now?" Peter, the impetuous one, demands. "I will lay down my life for you."

"Will you," Jesus responds. "The cock will not crow, till you have denied me three times."

What a man was Peter—so strong in aspiration, so persistent in his determination to conquer his shortcomings!

What a man was Jesus, to call forth in Peter and the others, rough men all, the strength of character and understanding that would make them the instruments to bring His message to the world!

What a power in Jesus, that even now after nearly two thousand years, His name is above every other name! Though some men may deny His divinity, and others deny His very existence, declaring Him to be only a mythical and not a historical character, yet none can deny the power of His name, His example, and His teaching. And few there be who could deny the secret longing to be like Him.

It is difficult to reduce to an abstraction a personality so three-dimensional as Jesus. If He is not real there would seem to be little foundation for a belief that any of us can attain to Christhood. And the counterfeit (if Jesus is an abstraction) is better than the reality.

Truly, like the Greeks who came to Andrew at the time of the Passover, "we would see Jesus!" Not Christ only, but Christ made manifest, as an actual embodiment in human form as

Jesus. We long to see His nature manifest in men today, manifest (oh, most of all) in ourself—Christ in us, our hope of glory.

Christ in the head of everyone to whom I speak.

Christ in the mouth of every person who speaks to me.

Christ in the eye of every person who looks upon me.

Christ in the ear of everyone who hears me today.

—St. Patrick

Many Rooms

" 'LET not your hearts be troubled; believe in God, believe also in me. In my Father's house are many rooms; if it were not so, would I have told you that I go to prepare a place for you? And when I go and prepare a place for you, I will come again and will take you to myself, that where I am you may be also. And you know the way where I am going.'

"Thomas said to him, 'Lord, we do not know where you are going; how can we know the way?' Jesus said to him, 'I am the way, and the truth, and the life; no one comes to the Father, but by me. If you had known me, you would have known my Father also; henceforth you know him and have seen him.' "

In the Father's house (heaven) are many rooms (abiding places.)

We do not have to die to get into heaven, neither are we excluded from heaven by relinquishing the human body. We are in heaven whenever we are in the consciousness of the Father's presence, His wisdom, power, right adjustment, and sustaining love.

What does it mean to you to be in heaven? Does it mean the same thing to others whom you know intimately as it does to you? To the artist, would not a large part of heaven be the ability and opportunity to give full, free, satisfying expression to his art, and to be able to feel that others (some others at least) responded to and appreciated his efforts? To the mother, would it not mean in great degree the health, security, advancement, and welfare of her children? To the minister, would it not mean the ability to communicate Truth, to serve others in love and humble competence? To the lover, would it not mean oneness in recognition, acceptance, purpose, and understanding with the beloved?

Truly in heaven there are many abiding places, many states of consciousness, the finding, through infinitely various channels, of meaning, purpose, and fulfillment of life's creative urge.

"I go and prepare a place for you . . . that where I am you may be also," said the Master. Did He mean that we are to find that place which He has prepared for us only in another world, remote and apart from this? Surely He must have included that future abode of the Spirit in His meaning: but not that only, else why should He also have said, "The kingdom of God is in the midst of you," and "The kingdom of heaven is at hand," or "This generation will not pass away till all these things take place"?

Had not Jesus gone away from them, it is unlikely that the disciples and other followers would have done any mighty works. So long as He was with them, they naturally, almost inevitably, looked to His greater vision, strength, and power for the right outworking of problems that confronted them. When they had failed to heal one who was afflicted, and they asked why they had not been able to do what He did so promptly, He said plainly that it was because they had not the faith. They had faith in Him; they did not have faith in the power of God in themselves. It was not simply that He Himself should work wonders that He came to men, but that they should find in themselves a power, through God, like unto His own.

When men heard Him say, "I go to the Father," they interpreted this as foretelling His death and resurrection. Instead He was telling them plainly the secret of His power. "He who believes in me will also do the works that I do; and greater works than these will he do," was, like many other passages in Holy Writ, not simply a promise but an admonition. They must turn to God as He did.

God gives to all men not the same gifts but the same power, His power, and "all these are inspired by one and the same Spirit who apportions to each one individually as he wills," that is, according to his individual state of consciousness.

We dwell not so much in places as in states or condition. In the vast house of the Father, the all-inclusive realm of being, are divers states of consciousness. No two of us are in exactly the same stage of development. What is heaven to one might well be almost the opposite to someone else. Our habitual state of consciousness is, for the time in which we accept it, our abiding place. We dwell in thoughts and feelings, not in figures on a dial, nor geographical locations as such. Our states of consciousness determine times and places more than times and places determine states of consciousness.

So long as we are incarnate in this formative world, our body is our objective abiding place. It is the mansion of the soul, "a house not made with hands," which in the ultimate shall be, according to promise, "eternal in the heavens." Man's hold upon the body is tenuous. For the average person it is a transient dwelling comparable to the tents in which the children of Israel dwelt during the nomadic days before they became a nation. Tents were to give way to temples, and finally Solomon was to rebuild the temple in Jerusalem as an enduring place of meeting between God and man. This in turn was to give way to Jesus' conception of a temple whose pattern was in the heavens of God's infinite mind; a temple which if it were to be laid down in death should be re-formed spiritually.

Until man "comes in to go out no more," that is, until he incarnates the Christ consciousness, his body is fashioned and refashioned continually of the "dust [or substance] of the earth." The bodily abode is continually changing, continually dying and being reborn. The myriad little bodies of which it is fashioned are continually dying and being eliminated; continually being replaced as new ones are born, so that in less than a year every part except the skeletal framework is replaced—and even the bones themselves are renewed every seven years. When Paul said, "I die every day," he was voicing a scientific truth; and he might well have added—"and daily I am reborn."

These continual births and deaths are necessary so that the great work of attaining to perfection shall go on, and so that man shall not indefinitely perpetuate any imperfection. And what is true of the body is also true of us mentally and emotionally. We die, and survive, a thousand deaths. We die to old limitations and are born to new freedoms; to old fears and superstitions that we may be born to new faith and understanding. God will not suffer our foot to be moved from the forward and upward path of His divine appointing.

Truly in God's great house of being we dwell in many rooms, and always going before us, leading, guiding, and inspiring us to the attainments of the goal of our high calling in Christ, is the gentle Master, preparing, by His example and instructions, a place for us, that where He is, we may be also!

Build thee more stately mansions, O my soul,
As the swift seasons roll!
Leave thy low-vaulted past!
Let each new temple, nobler than the last,
Shut thee from heaven with a dome more vast,
Till thou at length art free,
Leaving thine outgrown shell by life's unresting
     sea! (Holmes)

The Greater Works

"BELIEVE me that I am in the Father and the Father in me: or else believe me for the sake of the works themselves.

"Truly, truly, I say to you, he who believes in me will also do the works that I do; and greater works than these will he do, because I go to the Father.

"Whatsoever you ask in my name, I will do it, that the Father may be glorified in the Son.

"If you ask anything in my name, I will do it."

To believe in Jesus Christ is to accept Him in two aspects. He is not only human as Jesus,

but divine as the Christ. We find inspiration in
His winsomely human nature. We find application in understanding of the Christ principle
which He wondrously expressed, and which exists and awaits expression in us all. It is the
recognition of this divine potential that enables
us to do the works that He did—and even
greater works.

Until we believe in (agree to, consent to,
or accept) this great teaching of the Master, we
close the door against the spiritual attainment
that it was His purpose to share with us. We
must consent to forgiveness, consent to being
healed, consent to prosperity, consent to our
own innate goodness and the innate goodness
in others, in order for these to come forth more
fully and richly.

And the works that Jesus did?

Of Himself he could do nothing, but the
Father within Him, said Jesus, He "does the
works." Long before the time of Jesus, Job was
to cry out that the things of God were "too
wonderful" for him; that they were beyond His
understanding. They still are. But not too wonderful for God, or for the nature of God within us, to accomplish. We are filled with awe-
some wonder as we contemplate the things that
Jesus did and try to imagine ourself doing such
mighty works.

We love to think of healing the sick, raising the dead, restoring sight to the blind, enabling the lame to walk, teaching and preaching as Jesus did. These are what we first think of, as "doing the works that Jesus did."

We might more prudently consider what made these manifestations of God's mighty power possible.

It isn't very hard, nor does it take very long, to accomplish most mighty works, when we are all ready for them—when we are prepared. We marvel at anything well, efficiently, expertly, graciously, easily done. We may well marvel at the preparation, the discipline, dedication, training that makes these results possible. Indeed, the application of spiritual or mental or material power and directed energy *back of the manifestation* may well excite our wonder the more. For we witness in most cases only a partial expression of the divine potential that makes the expression possible.

When we direct our attention toward actually being like Jesus, developing the inward resources of God's nature within us, we soon begin to realize that these mighty works within the inner man are far greater than any outward application of them. The application hinges upon our acceptance of and response to the nature of God, and trust in His love and willingness to let us be the channels of His expression. It may seem to aggrandize us to be such channels. Actually it means almost putting ourself (our mundane, human self) out of the way so that He may appear. This seems to have been the significance of John the Baptist's allusion to Jesus Christ when he said, "He must increase, but I must decrease." Charles Fillmore relates John the Baptist to "a high intellectual perception of Truth, but not yet quickened of Spirit." A highly developed intellect is often true in what it affirms, yet may be false in what it denies. John recognized his own limitations (of thought) but also recognized the greater (spiritual) perception of Jesus.

"Every man is the leading character in his own life's drama," and at one time or another he plays all the parts. The Bible story is history, the story of all of us in our journey from sense to soul. This plane of life in which we now dwell is the plane of experience in which we are to learn the application of universal principle to personal needs of growth. Sometimes we lose sight (or memory) of the principle, and need the inspiration of an example of the application of principle to fact, "the word made flesh."

Jesus Christ is the supreme example, the Wayshower and the Way.

With faith in you, Lord Christ, I press on to the attainment of the goal of my own high calling. In You I envision the fulfillment of what in God's sight I truly am, and am to be. From Your inspired words and life I learn to seek first God's kingdom which I know is within me, trusting that the outward signs of the inward grace will follow, without haste, without delay, without strain or contention, but in perfect ways and under grace. I act on faith, knowing that as I apply the understanding that I have, more will be given me.

The Counselor

"I WILL pray the Father, and he will give you another Counselor, to be with you for ever, even the Spirit of truth, whom the world cannot receive, because it neither sees him nor knows him; you know him for he dwells with you, and will be in you.

"I will not leave you desolate; I will come to you. Yet a little while, and the world will see me no more, but you will see me; because I live, you will live also. In that day you will know that I am in my Father, and you in me, and I in you."

John 16:7 sheds further light on this passage

about the Counselor, quoting Jesus as saying, "Nevertheless I tell you the truth: it is to your advantage that I go away, for if I do not go away, the Counselor will not come to you; but if I go, I will send him to you." And we are reminded that when Judas had protested Mary's use of a costly ointment of spikenard to anoint Jesus' feet, He had said, "The poor you always have with you, but you do not always have me."

As long as Jesus was with them, the disciples did no mighty works. His light was so bright that they could not see their own. It was important to them—indeed it is important to all of us—to find "the true light that lightens every man . . . coming into the world." We cannot walk very far by a borrowed light. Not even that of Jesus, much as we may love and adore Him. He would have us know the Counselor, even the Spirit of truth, that shall lead us into all understanding.

As long as Jesus was with them, the disciples depended upon Him to teach, to preach, to heal. They must find the light of God's nature within themselves, and let their own light shine.

He had promised them that whatever they should ask in His name, He would do—and the implication was that He would do it through them rather than for them; implication implicit in the promise too that they would ask wisely, for He said on one occasion, "You . . . do not receive, because you ask wrongly." To ask in His name was in effect to ask in His nature, and not in the name of the selfish nature that always wants its own way.

A story in point is that of two clerics of different denominations, seeking taxis at a crowded air terminal. Both started for the same cab at the same time. One of the clergymen turned to the other: "Why not share this cab together? After all, we are both serving the same Lord." "Yes," the second responded, "You in your way, and I in His."

We would all like to think that we are living and serving not in our way only, but in His. The testimony is in holding all desires firmly enough to be definite yet loosely enough to be amended.

"This, O God, is my good as I see it. Nevertheless I want what in your sight is best."

The Branch and
the Vine

"I AM the true vine, and my Father is the
vinedresser. Every branch of mine that bears no
fruit, he takes away, and every branch that does
bear fruit, he prunes, that it may bear more fruit.
You are already more clean by the word which
I have spoken to you. Abide in me, and I in you.
As the branch cannot bear fruit by itself, unless
it abides in the vine, neither can you, unless you
abide in me. I am the vine, you are the branches.
He who abides in me, and I in him, he it is that
bears much fruit, for apart from me you can do
nothing. If a man does not abide in me, he is
cast forth as a branch and withers; and the

branches are gathered, thrown into the fire and burned. If you abide in me, and my words abide in you, ask whatever you will, and it shall be done for you. By this my Father is glorified, that you bear much fruit, and so prove to be my disciples."

A modern-day Truth student went on a journey of fifteen hundred miles to take some lessons from a metaphysical teacher he had heard of. When he returned home his friends all wanted to know what he had learned from his course of study.

"Oh, it was wonderful!" he exclaimed.

"Yes, but what did you learn from it?" they persisted.

"It cost three hundred dollars for the tuition," he responded.

"But what did you learn for the three hundred dollars?"

"Well, if you must know, I learned that God and I are one, and He is the one!" the student declared.

In a single simple sentence he worded a tremendous realization. Really to know this is certainly worth three hundred dollars! Indeed, it is beyond price. And it involves much more than the payment of a sum of money. It involves perhaps a lifetime of living and learning, or even many lifetimes—or, if the student is all ready for the realization, it may seem so simple and easy to comprehend and to put into practice that it is accepted in a moment, in "the twinkling of an eye," to which Paul referred in another connotation.

Jesus used a graphic metaphor when He spoke of Himself as the true vine, God as the vinedresser.

For it is one thing to be one with God, and quite another thing to be consciously so. That we may become *consciously* that which in truth we are *eternally* is the goal of our attainment in this plane of life.

The branch, cut off from the vine, withers and dies. The stream cut off from the mountain lake that is its source trickles away to nothingness; an arm or a leg separated from its parent body becomes lifeless. Jesus used this symbolism at the last supper with His disciples.

We, if we could be separated from the Source of our being, could not live. We, not truly realizing our oneness with that Source, do not truly live, in the full meaning of that term, but merely exist.

The evidence that we truly know ourself to be a branch of the true vine is that our life exemplifies that knowledge. Our life becomes fruitful, significant, productive.

Bible commentators think of the true vine as

representing Israel and/or the true Israelites as His followers. But in the time of Jesus the Jewish people had long been without prophets and seers to stir their religious nature. They were like branches withering on the vine, like sheep without a shepherd, like a feeble stream no longer replenished from on high.

In our present time there are evidences of man's great need for a vital realization of oneness with God. The cynical assertion that God is dead has a certain degree of validity in reverse. For it is not God who is dead; rather, those who make the assertion are less spiritually alive than God meant us all to be. As a present-day cartoonist presented the notion in his syndicated feature: "God is not dead. He is merely unemployed."

In the present-day trend toward integration of racial groups—and the resistance to it—we might conjecture a relationship to every man's inner conflict between two sides of his nature: one that wants very much to be consciously one with the Creator and the created (even though the longing is submerged and only vaguely recognized) and the other that resists the concept of integration, either with God or man; motivated, possibly, by the fear that if he yields just a little he may lose himself entirely.

In the philosophy of Jesus it is the man who

yields little who loses. "He who finds his life will lose it, and he who loses his life for my sake will find it." The happiest men, and most content, are those who "lose themselves" as we say in devotion to family and friends, their country or their God.

I would be so consciously one with You, O loving Presence, that there is no barrier of partition between us. I cannot tell where You leave off and I begin. We are one, as You and the Father are one. My thoughts, my feeling, my words, my actions, my life, I dedicate to you. My life is Your life. Your energy flows in and through me as the bloodstream flows through my mortal body. I am continually renewed, restored, and vivified by Your life energy. I lose all sense of separateness from You, and in losing my life I find Your life.

I Have Called
You Friends

"GREATER love has no man than this, that a man lay down his life for his friends. You are my friends if you do what I command you. No longer do I call you servants, for the servant does not know his master's doing; but I have called you friends, for all that I have heard from my Father I have made known to you.

"You did not choose me, but I chose you and appointed you that you should go and bear fruit and that your fruit should abide; that whatever you ask the Father in my name, he may give it you.

"This I command you, to love one another."

"The Gospel began with friendship, and we know from common life what that is, and how it works," writes T. R. Glover in his book, "The Jesus of History."

As you read the words of Jesus—the so-called Sermon on the Mount in the fifth, sixth, and seventh chapters of Matthew, or the fourteenth and seventeenth chapters of John, for instance—do you get the feeling of an oration, a formal discourse such as you would picture in a church auditorium or a lecture hall today, with people, hundreds of them, sitting in stiff rows before the speaker? Do you not rather have the feeling of someone, a learned someone truly, but not stuffy, talking informally with friends whom he loves, and with whom he longs to share his inmost, loftiest, and most meaningful thoughts?

He is not talking down to them, nor up to them in some kind of reverse condescension, but across, as between equals. With Jesus we get no sense of flowery phrases, no grandiloquent language whose intent would be to impress rather than to communicate. Instead He talks in terms of things that are familiar to them all: fishes, and boats, and the sea; foxes and their holes, birds and their nests, sheep and shepherds, and farmers tilling the soil, sowing the seed, watching the sky for signs of needed rainfall; yeast and dough and bread, patches on worn garments, wine and wineskins, wares of the marketplace, treasures lost and found.

But by the turn of a phrase, like turning a gem so that the sunlight reveals its hidden fire, He gives familiar things new meaning, so that "All spoke well of him, and wondered at the gracious words which proceeded out of his mouth."

The disciples come to Him with situations that trouble them. He respects their personalities. He does not silence them with an obscure axiom.

He finds time for them. "I have prayed for you." He lets them do things for Him, manage the boat on a troubled sea, go ahead and prepare the Passover, watch with Him and pray with Him in the times of His own troubled thoughts. He shows His trust in them: "All things that I have heard of my Father I have made known unto you."

He leads men into the kingdom not by oratory or feats of magic or esoteric philosophy, but by friendship and by love. To the present age when men seek to avoid involvement, when like the priest and the Levite in the old story of the good Samaritan, we are tempted to pass by other people's troubles (if indeed that is possible in a world growing ever smaller, and nations and races coming ever closer and closer

whether they like it or not), the winsome
Teacher of Galilee has a message, that might
be both the challenge and the answer for this
time: "I have called you friends."

O Friend,
You have been such a friend to me,
I come into Your presence
Thought-stained from the world.
The banners of my spirit dragging in earth-dust.
Then suddenly all this is as nothing.
It does not matter any longer,
For in the calm peace of Your presence
The worn garment of much-troubled thought
Slips from my shoulders.
I seem clothed anew in shining raiment.

Knowing and Doing

" 'As THE Father has loved me, so have
I loved you; abide in my love. If you keep my
commandments, you will abide in my love, just
as I have kept my Father's commandments and
abide in his love. These things I have spoken to
you, that my joy may be in you, and that your
joy may be full. This is my commandment, that
you love one another as I have loved you.' "

" 'Teacher, which is the great commandment in the law?' And he said to him, 'You
shall love the Lord your God with all your heart,
and with all your soul, and with all your mind.
This is the great and first commandment. And a

second is like it, you shall love your neighbor as yourself. On these two commandments depends all law and the prophets.' "

If we fall short of the goal of "the upward call of God in Christ Jesus"—to use Paul's words—and in all honesty it must be admitted that we do—the falling short may be said to be not so much in failure to know, as in failure to fulfill what we know. As Shakespeare has Portia say in "The Merchant of Venice": "If to do were as easy as to know what were good to do, chapels had been churches, and poor men's cottages princes' palaces. It is a good divine that follows his own instructions: I can easier teach twenty what were good to be done, than to be one of the twenty to follow mine own teaching." Or as Thomas, Cardinal Wolsey lamented, "Had I but served God as diligently as I have served the King, he would not have given me over in my gray hairs."

None of us in our human nature knows all that there is to know, indeed not all that we feel we need to know. Yet the one sure way to increase our knowledge and consequent feeling of adequacy, is to put what we do know to the test of experience.

In this age of sophistry we are often confronted by the comment, even the appraisal, "Unity is so simple," by which we assume the speaker to mean that practical Christianity is simple. We must agree. In less than thirty words Jesus stated the two commandments upon which "depends all the law and the prophets." Simple, yes. But have we found it very easy? If we have to stop and appraise every action, every thought and feeling, every word, and consider whether in them we are putting God first, it is pretty evident that we are not.

To dwell so constantly in the sense of God's presence that our response to people's thoughts and actions, and to situations that confront us, is spontaneously constructive and loving is a discipline that is surely a lifetime project. Perhaps, put this way, it sounds laborious and depressing. Yet there are those who work at it consistently who tell us that every successful effort is rewarding. This is something for which one cannot *be* rewarded. The reward is in the doing.

How shall we love the Lord with all our heart, mind, and soul? There are as many ways as there are circumstances. When we are faced by a strong difference of viewpoint in the person of someone with whom we have dealings, humanly we want our own views to be justifed, humanly we find it difficult to accept an opposing view. Can we then reach to an attitude of mind and heart in which we affirm, *"All things conform to the right thing, under grace and perfect law"?* When the human nature cries out against delays and demands instant fulfillment, can we affirm right outcome *"without haste nor delay, in perfect ways and under grace"?* When we are under threat of some deprivation, can we confidently know that *"Nothing can take from me what God has for me,"* or accept God's assurance to Joel, "I will restore to you the years which the swarming locust has eaten"?

Over and over we are brought to the realization that it is not just what we know (or more accurately, know about) but what we do about what we know, that makes us effective, practical Christians.

Deeply within me, I know the Truth. I discern it readily and apply it easily. There is an inner guide that offers me instruction and inspiration, a guide that sometimes I call the I Am, sometimes my Higher Self, sometimes the Innate, and most often the Christ. I give thanks that He guides me now, and always will. I ask Him to make His guidance very clear and plain to me so that I shall not mistake it, because sometimes I feel like a little child, not knowing how to go out or come in: but with Him the darkness is as the light, and crooked places are made straight, and somehow by His grace all things work, and are now working, together for good.

Yet Many Things

"I HAVE yet many things to say to you, but you cannot bear them now. When the Spirit of truth comes, he will guide you into all the truth; for he will not speak of his own authority, but whatever he hears he will speak, and he will declare to you the things that are to come."

The eager student is likely to feel disappointed by this statement of Jesus, "you cannot bear them now." We want to know everything, do everything, be all things that in the fullness of our higher nature it is intended that we shall be. If we are as wise as we are avid for Truth, we will strive, with Paul, in whatsoever state we find ourself, to be content—not satisfied, truly, but content.

Let patience have its perfect work. Savor the lessons and opportunities that are at hand. Learn of them, both the ones you cherish and those you tend to shun.

All through the teachings of Jesus there is an undertone, and frequently an overt tone, of what the people of the East call karma, or what we of the Western world call cause and effect.

Though we enter this world in the guise of helpless infants, the infancy is more apparent than real. Our life did not begin when we came here, nor does it end by our leaving this plane of being. Life is a continuum. A lifetime is only a segment of a larger life. We have brought with us, stored in the subconscious, the experiences of times long past, lessons learned or to be learned, obligations to be fulfilled, projects to be worked out in the present and in the relatively near future. They are stored away in the subconscious and therefore only partly recognized in the conscious mind, because they would be too much for us to hold in conscious memory all at once. They would occupy so large a place in our consciousness that we would have little time or energy for anything else. We could not bear them yet, or all at once.

Somehow the connotation of the expression,

"bear them," suggests something difficult or
ominous, the way many people feel about the
will of God. In neither case is this feeling justified. Both involve change. Both involve growth.
But change is natural, even inevitable; at most
it can be only delayed, and often inadvisably.
Growth is essential too, and it is good. But too
much of either one, too soon, and all at once,
can be overwhelming. Even Jesus in the garden
of Gethsemane prayed, "If it be possible, let
this cup pass from me," and in this we anticipate
the Cross. (Oddly, we do not seem to anticipate
the Resurrection.)

"Bear them" suggests problems, and of
problems we feel that we have enough. "Ready
for them" would be better. "Grasp them" is
Doctor Lamsa's translation, and this seems con-
sonant with the over-all purpose of Jesus' ministry.

If He were to appear corporeally to us in
the world today as He did in Palestine should
we be ready for the "many things" that He had
still to tell the disciples before He left them?
We are eager to know them, we say: and even as
we say it, we realize that He gave us a way to
know them. The Counselor would come, He
told us, even the Spirit of truth, and He would
lead us into all the truth. The way is simple; it
is not quite as easy as it sounds, but it is sure,

and once upon the path we have only to keep
going forward. Sometimes we would like to go
more rapidly. Sometimes the pace of events
seems too swift.

The experiences we have from day to day
are, by a divine but not obvious plan, designed
to prepare us for greater things to come. "Without haste, without delay, in perfect ways and
under grace."

*I am in stride with the upward, progressive
movement of life, and the mark of success is
upon me. This, O loving Presence, I seek to
make as true in fact as it is true in principle.
But I neither rush nor lag. I am attuned to my
own soul's need. It sets its own pace, and all
things conform. With the poet, I too say:*

"I stay my haste, I make delays,
  For what avails this eager pace?
  I stand amid th' eternal ways
  And what is mine shall know my face.
  The stars come nightly to the sky,
  The tidal wave unto the sea,
  Nor time, nor space, nor deep, nor high
  Can keep my own away from me."

From Sorrow to Joy

"THEY said, 'What does he mean by "a little while"? We do not know what he means.'

"Jesus knew that they wanted to ask him: so he said to them, 'Is this what you are asking yourselves, what I meant by saying, "A little while, and you will not see me, and again a little while, and you will see me"? Truly, truly, I say to you, you will weep and lament, but the world will rejoice; and you will be sorrowful, but your sorrow will turn into joy. When a woman is in travail she has sorrow, because her hour has come; but when she is delivered of the child, she no longer remembers the anguish, for joy that a child is born into the world. So you have sorrow now, but I will see you again, and your hearts will rejoice, and no one will take your joy from you."

It is characteristic of Jesus that the figures of speech He used were never trite or hackneyed. At least not when he used them. If they seem so now, it is because they have been so often quoted. So instead of quoting the Psalmist, that "weeping may tarry for the night, but joy comes with the morning," we find Him comparing His approaching travail and that of the disciples to the suffering of a woman in childbirth, and even those who do not or could not experience giving birth to a child are nonetheless captured by the graphic nature of His words.

Oh yes, we exclaim. We can understand. We have had our own painful experiences; and we have known the blessed release and freedom we have felt when the worst was over. Did we ever before so appreciate normal bodily functioning, a mind and heart free from the ache of some sorrow? Wonderful is the love of friends and family, the warmth of the sunlight, the ability to walk freely beneath the bright sky!

"You will feel sad because I will be away from you for a while," Jesus is telling His disciples, "and you may experience the scorn of My enemies who will rejoice in what they think of as My failure. But I will return (through the resurrection, and also as an enduring spirit in you which none may dispel) and your sorrow will be turned into joy." .

So it often is with those of us today who seek to follow, though afar, in the Master's footsteps. Our troubles are as pebbles in the road, the blessings we shall gain are as the everlasting hills.

We are like the little grandmother who came to her pastor with a list of ills. "There are five things the matter with me," she declared. "And how many things are all right with you?" he responded. With a look of surprise she exclaimed, "They're beyond number for counting!"

Looking back upon a time of challenge that we have experienced, it is difficult to remember the intensity of pain, the depth of despair. They endured for the night of our affliction, but with the dawn they are gone. There is no more life in them. Suffer it to be so. Let the dead past bury its dead. Go forward in the new day of conquest and overcoming.

Let me remember and trust in the assurance, O loving Presence, that You are with me in the dark hours as in the dawn; that there is wonder-working power in the sustaining faith that "This too shall pass." Let me be strong in the realization that the soul has its birth-pangs too, and rejoice in the birth to new strength, a new sense of adequacy and purpose. Let me remember your inspiriting words, "Your sorrow will turn to joy," and claim them as my own.

Ask and Receive

" 'In that day you will ask nothing of me.
Truly, truly, I say to you, If you ask anything of
the Father, he will give it to you in my name.
Hitherto you have asked nothing in my name;
ask, and you will receive, that your joy may be
full.

" 'I have said this to you in figures; the hour
is coming when I shall no longer speak to you
in figures, but tell you plainly of the Father. In
that day you will ask in my name; and I do not
say to you that I shall pray the Father for you;
for the Father himself loves you, because you
have loved me and have believed that I come

from the Father. I came from the Father and have come into the world; again, I am leaving the world and going to the Father.'

"His disciples said, 'Ah, now you are speaking plainly, not in any figure! Now we know that you know all things, and need none to question you; by this we believe that you came from God.' "

To ask in the name of Jesus Christ is to ask in the nature of Jesus Christ. When that nature is confirmed in us, we will not ask amiss, but in all righteousness, or right purpose, and our requests will be fulfilled. But unless the truth is in us as a working factor in our life, it will not seem to be so. We can only receive what we are prepared to receive. We must stir up the gift of God that is within us.

Perhaps the greatest stumblingblock for the disciples—and the greatest one for us today—is that we expect God to do something *for* us that needs to be done *through* us.

Jesus' teachings about the giving of alms "in secret" is still puzzling to many. Even those who have read the Lloyd C. Douglas novel "Magnificent Obsession" often fail to grasp the principle involved, and think of it as just a story; whereas what Jesus was saying, and what Douglas tried to make clear in the dramatic action of his story, is that when we make God our partner in giving, and do not give that we "may be praised by men," the Father "who sees in secret" will reward us openly. This takes giving out of the element of barter ("You must give to me because I have given to you") and puts it in its higher category of giving because it is a good, even a Godlike, thing to do, let results be what they may.

The hazard in asking for anything less than the will of God is that we are so very likely to get what we ask for; and what we ask for takes its pattern not exclusively from our stated prayers or our wishful thinking, but from our habitual responses to life. If a man affirms health in his prayers, and illness by his way of life, which, should we say, is the more likely—even inevitably—to be answered? Our own unconscious recognition of this imbalance between aspiration and activation is found in the expression, "You asked for it!"

My whole being, body, mind, soul, spirit, asks for your guidance, O God. I ask for a healthy body by observing the laws of health as I know them. I ask for wisdom by exercising my mental aptitudes, by enlarging my knowledge of things supernal and mundane. I let "this mind [be in me which was also] in Christ Jesus." I feel my oneness with Him, and my soul is enriched, renewed, and restored. From the center of light within me, O God, I radiate love and healing to all the world. I give thanks that all that is mind by divine right comes to me in response to Your presence within me.

The Hour Has Come

"WHEN Jesus had spoken these words, he lifted up his eyes to heaven and said, 'Father, the hour has come; glorify thy Son that the Son may glorify thee, since thou hast given him power over all flesh, to give eternal life to all whom thou hast given him. And this is eternal life, that they know thee the only true God, and Jesus Christ whom thou hast sent.

'I glorified thee on earth, having accomplished the work which thou gavest me to do; and now, Father, glorify thou me in thy own presence with the glory which I had with thee before the world was made.' "

"The hour has come," and "for this purpose I have come to this hour," said Jesus. The connotation is depressing if we think only of the immediately related events. It is reassuring, even inspiring to one who looks beyond the immediate to the ultimate. "There is nothing so powerful as an idea whose time has come," declared the poet Goethe. The life of Jesus was the embodiment of a world-changing idea.

A part of the greatness of Jesus was that He not only had and recognized a purpose in His life, but followed through to its fulfillment.

There is a purpose for the life of each one of us. Some of us seem to sense this even before we can define it. And so we may say, as we face some climactic experience, "For this [hidden] purpose I have come to this hour." To have the conviction that there is a divine destiny which, as the poet says, "shapes our ends, rough hew them how we will," can be very comforting and reassuring. In such a conviction we are reaching past time into eternity, wherein cause and effect, idea and expression, are not separated as they appear to be, but are one.

Cultivate a feeling for this truth and it will bring you increased confidence, a sense of adequacy, of purpose. Say, and let it be not from your intellect alone but from your heart: *"For this purpose was I brought to this time, this place, this hour. By God's grace I am always in the right place at the right time, doing the right thing in the right way."*

Such a realization is like a call to the universe. It helps to put us in tune with universal forces, and most especially to align us with the purposes we are to serve, the lessons we are to learn, the blessings we are to receive, enjoy, and share with others.

Does this mean, then, that the path of our life is predetermined, that we have no choice in such matters? We have a destiny that is like the destination of a ship on a long sea voyage. The path of the ship may vary due to weather, but its direction is set. The passengers have considerable freedom—the freedom of the ship, but not of the sea.

Time is a characteristic of this plane of life in which "for a time" we dwell. We come to (that is, we approach) experiences in consciousness. Our recognition of purpose, our feeling of intent, evokes the declaration, "The hour has come," or "There is a good purpose that brings me to this hour, this experience." Apparently the Psalmist recognized this concept when he cried:

"Open to me the gates of righteousness,
    that I may enter through them and give
    thanks to the LORD.

This is the gate of the LORD;
 the righteous shall enter through it.
This is the LORD'S doing;
 it is marvelous in our eyes.
This is the day which the LORD has made;
 let us rejoice and be glad in it.
Thou art my God, and I will give thanks to thee;
 thou art my God, I will extol thee."

Gethsemane

"AND they went to a place which was
called Gethsemane; and he said to his disciples,
'Sit here, while I pray.' And he took with him
Peter and James and John, and began to be
greatly distressed and troubled. And he said to
them, 'My soul is very sorrowful, even to death;
remain here, and watch.' And going a little
farther, he fell on the ground and prayed that,
if it were possible, the hour might pass from
him. And he said, 'Abba, Father, all things are
possible to thee; remove this cup from me; yet
not what I will, but what thou wilt.'

"And he came and found them sleeping, and he said to Peter, 'Simon, are you asleep? Could you not watch one hour? Watch and pray, that you may not enter into temptation; the spirit indeed is willing, but the flesh is weak.'

"And again he went away and prayed, saying the same words. And again he came and found them sleeping, for their eyes were very heavy; and they did not know what to answer him.

"And he came the third time, and said to them, 'Are you still sleeping and taking your rest? It is enough: the hour has come; the Son of man is betrayed into the hands of sinners. Rise, let us be going; see, my betrayer is at hand.' "

Spring comes with a rush of splendor in Palestine; and gardens, beautiful everywhere in spring, are especially so there, when the deep pink of almond blossoms blends with the mousy gray of olive branches and the yellow-green of new shoots on the fig trees. Lovely in the warm light of the sun; tenderly beautiful when night has lighted her tapers and set a silver lantern in the sky. The almond flowers glow faintly in the moonlight; the little olive leaves send long, slender fingers of shade across the garden path; shade that, troubled, deepens as restless clouds veil the moon.

There is another shadow in the garden, too
—a shadow that moonlight and tree shape could
not fashion; the dark shadow of a cross that
rests over the Son of God.

It is very quiet in the garden; a quiet broken
only by the mournful cry of a night bird; the
tiny rustling of shattered blossoms that form a
spring blanket for the leafy earth, the even
tinier rustlings of tiniest crawling, creeping
life, and the occasional deep breath of human
slumberers.

A man has come to the garden. He has come
to rest and to pray. And though He is the Son
of God, master of heaven and earth, with such
inward light as no other has yet revealed, for
the time He is, quite simply I think, the gentle
Jesus, brother of men, bowed beneath such a
weight of human woe as only great hearts can
feel, and come to a quiet garden to lie prone
against the only breast that can bear His sorrows' weight. There is comfort in remembering
that this great, strong Man of God turned to
Mother Earth, as lesser men have done, when
His trouble seemed too big to carry or to share.

He, who had healed hundreds of their woes
of mind and body, who had suffered a wretched
woman to pour out her tears upon His feet,
found Himself alone in Gethsemane. There had
been many to share His blessings. There was

none to share His sorrow. The people of His
own village had long since turned from Him.
The priests and scribes were leagued against
Him. The loyalty of the populace was wavering;
already one of the Twelve had gone secretly to
betray Him. Even Peter, James, and John, whom
He had asked to watch with Him through the
night, could not so much as keep awake.

He had to face His greatest test alone.

As with the Master, so it is with lesser men:
in the most soul-searching tests of the spirit, we
must stand alone—alone with God.

In the garden of Gethsemane, Jesus faced
the hardest problems that men have to meet—
hatred, jealousy, rejection, betrayal, defeat,
physical suffering, death, and (perhaps worst
of all) human loneliness. It was the human
Jesus from whom the cry was wrung, "My
Father, if it be possible, let this cup pass from
me; nevertheless, not as I will, but as thou wilt."
It was Jesus renewed in power and courage,
reaching past the dark shadow into the everlasting light, who said ever so gently to poor,
drowsy Peter, "So, could you not watch with
me one hour? . . . the spirit indeed is willing,
but the flesh is weak." It was Jesus the Christ,
once more the radiant Son of God, who added,
"Are you still sleeping and taking your rest?
. . . the hour is at hand," and, to the others,

"Rise, let us be going; see, my betrayer is at hand."

You and I, all of us, have what we might describe as our Gethsemanes. We may even have what have been described as our "crucifixions." It takes a courageous man, however, to place his lesser woes beside that picture of Gethsemane, and see his troubles shrink. It takes a wise and faithful man to go one step further; to face his own Gethsemane alone with God, and to call forth the faith that sees beyond crucifixion to resurrection.

If we go so far as to compare our experiences to Gethsemane and Calvary, we should go further: to the resurrection. Do not stop part way. Go the whole way. And the whole way is past apparent defeat into ultimate victory.

With enlightened vision I see that only the good is enduringly true; all that is less than good that God has for me comes not to endure, but comes to pass. I know that what God wills for me, He also helps me to fulfill, and that His will for me is good, good beyond my present understanding. So I pray that where I do not clearly see, I shall have faith to place my hand in that of our dear Christ until faith has grown to sight, and darkness gives way to dawn—the dawn of ever-expanding insight and understanding.

In Times of Trial

"So THE band of soldiers and their captain and the officers of the Jews seized and bound him. First they led him to Annas; for he was the father-in-law of Caiaphas, who was the high priest that year. It was Caiaphas who had given counsel to the Jews that it was expedient that one man should die for the people.

"Simon Peter followed Jesus, and so did another disciple. As this disciple was known to the high priest, he entered the court of the high priest along with Jesus, while Peter stood outside the door. So the other disciple, who was known to the high priest, went out and spoke

to the maid who kept the door, and brought
Peter in. The maid who kept the door said to
Peter, 'Are not you also one of this man's disciples?' He said, 'I am not.' Now the servants
and officers had made a charcoal fire, because
it was cold, and they were standing and warming themselves; Peter also was with them, standing and warming himself.

"The high priest then questioned Jesus about
his disciples and his teaching. Jesus answered
him, 'I have spoken openly to the world; I have
always taught in synagogues and in the temple,
where all Jews come together; and I have said
nothing secretly. Why do you ask me? Ask
those who have heard me, what I said to them;
they know what I said.'

"When he had said this, one of the officers
standing by struck Jesus with his hand, saying,
'Is that how you answer the high priest?' Jesus
answered him, 'If I have spoken wrongly, bear
witness to the wrong; but if I have spoken
rightly, why do you strike me?'

"Annas then sent him bound to Caiaphas
the high priest."

Very early on Friday morning of that week
that changed the world, Jesus was brought before Annas, in the first of the trials, mockeries
all of them, that surely in the inner sight of
Jesus were a kind of minor accompaniment to

the major theme of His purpose and its fulfillment. Peter and the other disciples were non-
plused by Jesus' nonresistant attitude in facing
revilement, rejection, and abuse.

No one but Jesus Himself could see beyond these torturous events—at least no further
than crucifixion. Only Jesus could see that they
were but the shadows preceding a great light;
that beyond the dark hours there would be
resurrection and ascension; that these lesser,
painful things were only the preludes to the
accomplishment of His divine mission.

"Put your sword back into its place," He
admonishes Peter, "for all who take the sword
will perish by the sword. Do you think that I
cannot appeal to my Father, and he will at once
send me more than twelve legions of angels?"
He had more than Himself to serve, and did so
with supreme poise and self-abnegation.

It is a temptation here to expand upon the
hidden teachings of Jesus, the ancient wisdom.
He knew, He taught, the truth that every jot
and tittle of spiritual law must be fulfilled. Obviously all they who take the sword are not
slain by the sword *in the same lifetime.* Life is
a continuum, a serial rather than a short story.
If our accounts are not settled in one lifetime,
they will be in another.

And Jesus, as a master of that ancient wis-

dom, would not use it selfishly, to save Himself
at the expense of others. By the grace of God
and His own spiritual power, He could indeed
command spiritual forces to protect Himself
against His enemies. It was not because He
lacked power, but because He had great spiritual wisdom, purpose, and compassion, that He
did not do so.

So He is brought before Annas, who had
been a high priest before his son-in-law Caiaphas succeeded him. As a judge, Annas had no
right to make a case against Jesus by His own
words. But Annas was not so much a judge as
he was an *agent provocateur* who had already
condemned Jesus before questioning Him as to
His disciples and His doctrine.

"I have had no secret meetings," says Jesus
in effect. "I have taught openly to the world,
even in the synagogues where the Jews assemble.
Do not ask me. Ask anyone who has heard me,
what I have taught."

Things weren't going as Annas wanted. One
of the soldiers, seeing this, struck Jesus with
the palm of his hand. Again Jesus' response was
unanswerable: "If I have spoken wrongly, bear
witness to the wrong; but if I have spoken
rightly, why do you strike me?" An impartial
judge would have seen the validity of Jesus'
words. But Annas was not seeking justice. He

had already pronounced judgment in his mind.

What is helpful and inspiring in reviewing these events? Inspiration, certainly, in the courage and patience of Jesus. For our own aspiration to be more like Him, there is this: In times of trial relate the experience to the larger purpose of your life.

A teacher endeavored to comfort a young woman who had had grievous reverses, disheartening experiences with persons whom she had trusted. "You have gone through a lot," the teacher commented. The woman's response was emphatic: "I want you to know that I have not merely gone through a lot. I have come through a lot!" She had, indeed, and had attained a victory. Her ultimate achievements far exceed those for which she had aimed and been defeated. ·

I have seen the turning of the tides. I have seen the changing of the seasons. I have seen calm after storm. I have seen the miracle healing of a wound. Oh, let me find the patience not simply to endure, but rather to know that when the tide goes out it will return, that winter's blast will yield to summer's bounty, and storms give way to peace. Let me learn, then, in the midst of things immediate to relate to things eternal. O God, let me be steadfast in trial, and know that all things come right.

The Son of Man's
Appearing

"NOW the chief priests and the whole council sought false testimony against Jesus that they might put him to death, but they found none, though many false witnesses came forward. At last two came forward and said, 'This fellow said, "I am able to destroy the temple of God, and to build it in three days." '

"And the high priest stood up and said, 'Have you no answer to make? What is it that these men testify against you?' But Jesus was silent. And the high priest said to him, 'I adjure you by the living God, tell us if you are the Christ, the Son of God.' Jesus said to him,

'You have said so. But I tell you, hereafter you will see the Son of man seated at the right hand of Power, and coming on the clouds of heaven.' "

Jesus Christ was indeed the prophet of the new age that is dawning upon the world. With the smashing of the atom, mankind has entered upon an era of such greatly accelerated progress that old ways of thinking about the nature of matter, of mankind, and our purpose in existence must undergo tremendous changes. In possibly more ways than we can yet foresee Jesus was the Wayshower and the Way. Certainly His concept of Himself, of God, of mankind, and of the powers within man and in nature were of a transcendent character.

It was neither boast nor fantasy that when He was asked, "What sign have you to show us for doing this?" He answered, "Destroy this temple, and in three days I will raise it up."

Apparently Jesus was aware of and proficient in the use of inherent powers of mind over matter . . . powers that mankind is becoming increasingly aware of, but as yet is able to apply only in such comparatively rare instances that they are still viewed with some skepticism by many scientists and psychologists. In the two-thousand-year cycle since Jesus first taught and demonstrated "the power of the spirit in

the inward man," manifest in healing the sick,
raising the dead, and in His own dramatic
resurrection, mankind is coming full circle to a
reaffirmation of these powers. What was once
considered "miracle" or "magic" is in process
of becoming the incipient science of the atomic
age.

That the "too, too solid flesh" of Shakespeare's description is anything but solid, we
already know. How to manipulate the minute
centers of light and energy of which matter is
composed has been discovered initially in the
most violent of ways—through atomic fission
and fusion. Experiments with the laser beam in
certain forms of corrective surgery have already
been made successfully. That the forms of matter may be changed by the understanding and
disciplined mind of a Christ-man apparently
was demonstrated by Jesus in His time: "the
first fruits" of man's cyclic return to the faith
that has been accepted because on occasion it
was effective, and shall be accepted because it
is understood.

Certainly Unity has been a prominent factor
in this "return" to "simple" but transcendent
primitive Christianity.

Charles Fillmore, back in 1927, wrote:
"Science has broken into the atom and revealed
it to be charged with tremendous energy that

may be released and may be made to give the inhabitants of the earth powers beyond expression, when its law of expression is discovered.

"Jesus evidently knew about this hidden energy in matter and used His knowledge to perform so-called miracles."

So Jesus' assertion, "You will see the Son of man seated at the right hand of Power, and coming on the clouds of heaven," begins to have a literal as well as a symbolical significance to the exploring, aspiring nature of present-day man.

We have seen the sons of men (*sons* with a small *s*) sitting on the right hand of power, and coming in the clouds of the heavens; and we may well pray that this can be a symbol of the nature of the Son of man, learning to apply the innate power of the spirit within; appearing in and dispelling the clouds that have obscured his understanding of the kingdom that Jesus admonished him to seek.

I have faith in God and His power now guiding the world, its leaders, its institutions, its people. I have faith in the world and its destiny. I have faith that the power of God is mightier than any seeming power that threatens the forces of right. I have faith that my own good and the good of those dear to me is precious in His sight, and that even now the forces of good surround, enfold, and protect us. I have faith in God to strengthen me, to guide and help me in doing whatever in His sight is wise and right and best, to fulfill the world's divine destiny—and my own.

Peter, the Impetuous

"NOW Peter was sitting outside in the courtyard. And a maid came up to him, and said, 'You also were with Jesus the Galilean.' But he denied it before them all, saying, 'I do not know what you mean.'

"And when he went out to the porch, another maid saw him, and she said to the bystanders, 'This man was with Jesus of Nazareth.' And again he denied it with an oath, 'I do not know the man.'

"After a little while the bystanders came up and said to Peter, 'Certainly you are also one of them, for your accent betrays you.' Then he began to invoke a curse on himself and to swear, 'I do not know the man.' And immediately the cock crowed. And Peter remembered the saying of Jesus, 'Before the cock crows, you will deny me three times.' And he went out and wept bitterly."

After Jesus' arrest on that Thursday night following the prayer in Gethsemane, He was forced to appear before Annas and Caiaphas. Peter and "another disciple" (as John refers to himself) had followed on the fringe of the crowd that was attracted by the occasion. When they came to the residence of Annas, John was permitted to enter, as he was known to the high priest. Peter, however, was excluded, and stood without. Shivering, from inward trepidation no doubt as well as from the chill of that darkest hour before dawn, he was attracted toward a fire of coals that some of the servants had started in the courtyard of the dwelling. As they were warming themselves around the fire Peter was three times asked if he was one of Jesus' disciples. Three times he declared that he was not, the third time in a burst of cursing and swearing. Just then Jesus was led across the courtyard in time to hear His most impetuous disciple declare that he never knew Him.

Peter shrank back from the Master's gaze, as the cock crowed to announce the first rays of

Friday morning's sun.

Peter remembered how, at the close of their supper, Jesus had told them that He would be leaving them, and that where He was to go they could not come. "Why cannot I follow you now? I will lay down my life for you" he cried. And Jesus had responded, "Will you lay down your life for me? Truly, truly, I say to you, the cock will not crow, till you have denied me three times."

"And he went out and wept bitterly."

Peter, so strong in aspirations, so many times weak in measuring up to them! How like the weaver, in Shakespeare's "A Midsummer Night's Dream." In the play-within-the-play, when the tradesmen of the village wanted to honor the Duke's wedding, they had determined to present the tragicomedy "Pyramus and Thisby." Nick Bottom wanted to play all the parts. He wanted to be the hero, the heroine, the lion, the wall, the lantern. So it was with Peter. He wanted to play all the parts, to be "the best of anybody."

He sought to follow Jesus when He walked on the water—and sank.

He protested that Jesus should not wash his feet. "If I do not wash you, you have no part in me," Jesus answers. "Oh, Lord, not my feet only but also my hands and my head!" Peter cries.

He is puzzled about speculation among the populace as to who Jesus might have been in the past. He comes to Jesus with the comments that He might have been Elijah or Jeremiah or one of the prophets, even John the Baptist reborn in Him. It was not until the penetrating gaze of Jesus was fixed upon him with the question, "But who do you say that I am?" that it dawned on Peter that Jesus was really the Messiah, the Christ, Son of the living God.

In the garden of Gethsemane he could not keep awake during the hour's watch. Awakened when Jesus was arrested, he was aroused as well, and cut off the ear of one of the soldiers. Jesus had to restrain him, and undo the damage Peter had done.

And though, afterward, his good impulse was to follow Jesus, his courage failed.

How much of Peter there is in all of us! We want to be strong, faithful to the Truth we know. When by thought or word or act we fail to measure up to what we know in theory, our chagrin is great. We go over and over in thought what we might have said or done, how we might have presented ourself better. We like to think that we will never make the same mistake again, and are impatient because often our progress seems so much slower than we could wish.

It is good for us to remember that Jesus did not condemn Peter, and loved him still, loved him into becoming the great leader he was capable of being. We trust that He loves us too!

In the inmost nature of my being I see myself as God sees me, endued with power from on high, ever faithful to Him. In times of challenge I set myself, stand still, and behold the salvation of the Lord. Daily I am growing in steadfastness and allegiance to my divine potential. Daily I am becoming in manifestation more and more like what I am in Truth. I neither shrink from nor invite difficulty, but go my way, without haste nor delay, trusting that sufficient unto each day's demands are the resources by which to meet them.

Judas Iscariot

"WHEN Judas, his betrayer, saw that he was condemned, he repented and brought back the thirty pieces of silver to the chief priests and elders, saying, 'I have sinned in betraying innocent blood.' They said, 'What is that to us? See to it yourself.' And throwing down the pieces of silver in the temple, he departed; and he went and hanged himself.

"But the chief priests, taking the pieces of silver, said, 'It is not lawful to put them into the treasury, because they are blood money.' So they took counsel, and bought with them the potter's field, to bury strangers in. Therefore that field has been called the Field of Blood to this day.

"Then was fulfilled what had been spoken by the prophet Jeremiah, saying, 'And they took the thirty pieces of silver, the price of him on whom a price had been set by some of the Sons of Israel, and they gave them for the potter's field, as the Lord directed me.' "

Gradually it began to dawn in the disciples' consciousness that in Christ's kingdom of heaven there were to be none of the things which the Jews expected their hoped-for Messiah to secure for them.

It was a great blow to their personal ambition. The blow was severe to Judas, most of all. From a worldly point of view Judas was perhaps the shrewdest of the twelve. That he loved Christ we can reasonably believe. But from his standpoint Christ was making feeble use of His amazing powers. He might have had the riches of the world, the power of a Caesar, the homage of nations. Instead He spoke and acted as if He were wholly unconcerned about such considerations. To Judas this must have seemed dangerous dalliance. With the world almost in His grasp, the Master was likely to lose it from sheer inaction. Something must be done.

Judas conceived a daring—and as it proved,

fatal—plan. He would betray Jesus to the Romans, and thereby force Him to use His powers in His own defense. Judas had seen evidences of that power used for others. That Jesus, under the shadow of Roman torture and death, would refuse to invoke the wrath of God upon His persecutors probably did not occur to the worldly-minded Judas.

He went to the chief priests and sold the Master for thirty pieces of silver. It was a small sum. Judas undoubtedly could have gotten more had the betrayal money been his object. Desperately he was attempting to force upon Jesus the crown of the Jews. How little he understood the Master is shown in the miserable, tragic failure of his plan.

His ambition, for himself and for his Master, slew them both; for when Judas saw what his scheming had done, he rushed away and hanged himself.

In all loyalty to Christ, we can yet afford to grant to Judas our pity.

The grief of those who mourned at the cross of Christ was at least free of self-condemnation.

The suffering of the Master was, withal, the suffering of a Man triumphant.

The agony of Judas could know no palliation.

Judas, emblem of worldly desire, and Jesus, symbol of practical idealism, both died in ignominy; Judas by his own hand, Jesus at the hands of the Romans. But the dark hour of Jesus has been dissolved in the bright glory of Christ, while the dark hour of Judas has become even darker through the ages.

In every man dwells a potential Judas, in every man also a potential Christ. Christ must be quickened in us all. Judas, too, must be accorded his place with the other apostles, redeemed by our understanding of the principle which he represents. Judas must become the guardian and conserver of the precious life of Christ, rather than its betrayer. This is the desire of Christ in us.

Christ's Kingdom

"PILATE entered the praetorium again and
called Jesus, and said to him, 'Are you the King
of the Jews?' Jesus answered, 'You say this of
your own accord, or did others say it to you
about me?' Pilate answered, 'Am I a Jew? Your
own nation and the chief priests have handed
you over to me; what have you done?' Jesus
answered, 'My kingship is not of this world; if
my kingship were of this world, my servants
would fight, that I might not be handed over to
the Jews; but my kingdom is not from the
world.'

"Pilate said to him, 'So you are a king?' Jesus answered, 'You say that I am a king. For this I was born, and for this have I come into the world, bear witness to the truth. Every one who is of the truth hears my voice.' Pilate said to him, 'What is truth?' "

The kingdom of heaven is not so much a place as it is a way of seeing a place, or a feeling about it. We do not have to die (in the somatic sense) to enter the kingdom, nor are we excluded from it by dying. Entering the kingdom does mean dying to a certain way of thinking, feeling, acting, and being born to another. "Unless one is born anew, he cannot see the kingdom of God," said Jesus.

"My kingship is not of this world," "The kingdom of heaven is at hand," and "The kingdom of God is within you," all can help us to have a clearer concept of the nature of Christ's kingdom. We are in the kingdom when we are consciously one with God. We may perhaps think of ourself as being in heaven when we are consciously one with God. We may perhaps think of ourself as being in heaven when we are consciously one with our good, when we are physically well, financially prosperous, when we are loved and approved by those whose approbation we seek. And this is a part of what being in the kingdom can mean. Where we sometimes fall short is in the order of our seeking.

"Be not anxious, saying, 'What shall we eat?' or 'What shall we drink?' or 'What shall we wear?' For the Gentiles seek all these things; and your heavenly Father knows that you need them all. But seek first his kingdom and his righteousness, and all these things shall be yours as well," said Jesus.

Mark tells about how one time when the Pharisees and Sadducees were asking Jesus questions about His teachings and authority, one of the scribes was impressed by Jesus' wisdom, and asked, "Which commandment is the first of all?" And Jesus answered, " 'The Lord our God, the Lord is one; and you shall love the Lord your God with all your soul, and with all your mind, and with all your strength.' The second is this, 'You shall love your neighbor as yourself.' And the scribe said to him, 'You are right, Teacher; you have truly said that he is one, and there is no other but he; and to love him with all the heart, and with all the understanding, and with all the strength, and to love one's neighbor as oneself, is much more than all whole burnt offerings and sacrifices.' And when Jesus saw that he answered wisely, he said to him, 'You are not far from the kingdom of God.' "

It is as simple—and as difficult—as that.

God has given us all the things of this earth worthily to enjoy, and they are in themselves good, and good for us so long as we possess them with understanding, and keep them in their proper place, subject to the nature of God within us. The challenge is that sometimes the blessings of earth which are meant to serve us, possess us instead. Having them is not wrong. Being possessed by them can be, as the rich young ruler who came to Jesus was to discover. He assured Jesus that he had kept the commandments of Moses from his youth. "There is one thing more you might do," said Jesus, in effect. "Go, sell all you have, and give to the poor, and then come and follow me." And the young man went away sorrowfully, because he had many possessions—or, more accurately, many things possessed him.

"And Jesus looking upon him loved him."

Part of the charismatic charm of Jesus was His great understanding of people. He was Himself a young man, perhaps no older in years than the wealthy young ruler, but ages apart in spiritual insight. Had not Jesus met the temptations of worldly wealth and power? Was He not in all manners tempted like as we? Only so could He speak so much wisdom with so much understanding of people's wants and

needs. Truly He spoke not as the scribes and
Pharisees, but as one having authority! And
that authority was not only the authority of His
Christly nature but of His human allegiance to
it as well.

To reconcile the Within and the Without
is the great overcoming, what de Chardin calls
"this double thread," which we pray we shall
not break, but rather strengthen.

*Let me not be so filled with the thought of
heaven that I neglect or reject the privileges and
responsibilities of earth, nor so enthralled by
the powers and principalities of earth that I
lose sight of eternal values and verities. Let me
be a whole man. Let me have no other gods before You, O God.*

The Trial

"**A** PHARISEE in the council named Gamaliel, a teacher of the law, held in honor by all the people, stood up and ordered the men to be put outside for a while. And he said to them, 'Men of Israel, take care what you do with these men. . . . Keep away from these men, and let them alone; for if this plan or this undertaking is of men, it will fail; but if it is of God, you will not be able to overthrow them. You might even be found opposing God!'"

If Nicodemus and Joseph of Arimathea, who were secret followers of Jesus, were present at the early morning council in the palace of

Caiaphas, they may very well have put forward the same protestations that Gamaliel was to voice at a later time with regard to Peter and the apostles.

The members of the council were, in both instances, and more especially in the case of Jesus, "opposing God."

The trial, or trials, constituted a travesty of justice. They seem to have been held solely to exact from Jesus a confession that He was the Son of God, which could be called blasphemy and punishable by death. The earlier complaints against him were:

That He had violated the Sabbath,

That He had invoked the power of Satan to work miracles,

That He had ignored the custom of the Jewish fathers about the washing of hands before eating,

That He claimed the right to forgive sins,

That He condoned the sin of adultery, as in the case of the woman caught in the act,

That He consorted with disreputable or otherwise unacceptable persons.

None of these charges was introduced at the trials.

Quite simply, the ruling class of the Jews, the Sadducees, had decided that Jesus was a

danger to the established order of their doctrines, and for once the Pharisees, usually their
opponents and rivals, found common cause with
them and agreed that this Galilean prophet must
be gotten rid of.

What they did not see, and what is obscure
to many even to this day, is that they were actually abetting, though cruelly, the very cause
that they opposed. It was not their decision,
though it seemed to be, that brought Jesus to
the cross of Calvary. He Himself had made
that decision when He entered Jerusalem the
preceding Sunday morning. He went through
the trials like a man possessed—because He was
indeed a man possessed by a purpose and a
vision that not even those closest to Him shared.

When a man has a big enough sense of purpose he loses himself (yet finds a greater self)
in his absorption by or dedication to the purpose. A sculptor, working with hammer and
chisel, persuades the marble to reveal his dream.
He may bruise or cut himself in the process, he
may forget meals, neglect rest and sleep, yet
deem these discomforts of small account. His
purpose takes precedence over these things.

"He who finds his life will lose it, and he
who loses his life for my sake will find it,"
Jesus had said. And to this day His saying is
true. There is no guarantee that those who seek

to follow Him, to embody His teachings in their own life, shall be exempt from difficulties or challenges. Rather it makes these "trials" (which come whether we are trying to follow Him or not) seem worthwhile, and more than that. When the purpose is big enough, the problems incident to its accomplishment are small enough to bear with grace. Without a purpose, any problem is too big.

Lord, quicken in us the vision that enables us to look within the fleshly walls of our temporal dwellings and behold Thy Spirit there. Quicken in us the creative fire that stirs us to mighty endeavors, making the toil of self-resurrection a joy, as with infinite pains and infinite pleasures, through infinite experiences and infinite services, and infinite thoughts and words and deeds of love, we reveal Thy likeness within.

What We Decree

"SO WHEN Pilate saw that he was gaining nothing, but rather that a riot was beginning, he took water and washed his hands before the crowd, saying, 'I am innocent of this man's blood; see to it yourselves.' And all the people answered, 'His blood be on us and on our children!' Then he released for them Barabbas."

A young woman was brought to a Unity minister for counseling concerning a problem with which her family had been unable to help her. She had a compulsion to be continually washing her hands and arms. She felt as if she could never get them clean enough and had resorted to such strong caustic cleansers that her hands and forearms were a mass of sores. Probably most physicians and psychologists, even more than metaphysicians, know this pattern of human behavior.

That the unhappy young woman had a deep feeling of guilt was immediately obvious. That no amount of soap, water, and other physical applications could wash away that feeling was equally obvious, though not to her.

Shakespeare has Lady Macbeth attempting the same thing as our modern young woman. A doctor and a lady-in-waiting are observing her:

"What is it that she does now? Look, how she rubs her hands."

The attendant answers. "It is an accustomed action with her, to seem thus washing her hands: I have known her to continue in this a quarter of an hour."

The doctor says: "Hark! she speaks: I will set down what comes from her, to satisfy my remembrance the more strongly."

And then the famous cry, so often quoted, "Out, damned spot! out, I say! . . . What! will these hands ne'er be clean?"

As supposedly sophisticated and worldly a man as Pilate by a like action attempts to absolve himself of the guilt of being a party to the torture and death of Jesus. How many washings, O Pilate, would it take? And what of the populace that dared cry out, "His blood be on us and on our children!"

Could the populace really realize the consequences of their words? Has His blood indeed been upon them down through the years? Is there some means by which they are made to realize the fact? or do they cry, in the present day, "What have I done that this should come upon me?" with reference to some experience that may actually be in expiation of the guilt they have assumed? And if so, what is the answer?

Jesus Himself was to give it before the day was done: "Father, forgive them: for they know not what they do."

Was it to the consequences of their words that Jesus referred, when on the way to the cross, He cried, "Do not weep for me, but weep for yourselves and for your children"?

"You will decide on a matter, and it will be established for you," we read in the Book of Job. Sometimes we indeed decree hard things for ourself, harder perhaps than God would ever think of doing. And only our rising into a higher level of understanding, and acts that are the results of such understanding, really free us from our self-imposed burdens. Only that, and the acceptance of forgiveness.

In Your name and nature, O Lord Christ, I decree freedom from condemnations and recriminations. If You could forgive those who so cruelly mistreated You, so can I forgive those whom I feel have mistreated me. I decree forgiveness. I decree freedom. I decree light and truth and love. I decree understanding and free and easy communication.

Who Is King?

"UPON this Pilate sought to release him, but the Jews cried out, 'If you release this man, you are not Caesar's friend; everyone who makes himself a king sets himself against Caesar.'

"When Pilate heard these words, he brought Jesus out, and sat down on the judgment seat at a place called The Pavement, and in Hebrew, Gabbatha. Now it was the day of Preparation of the Passover; it was about the sixth hour. He said to the Jews, 'Here is your King!' They cried out, 'Away with him, away with him, crucify him!' Pilate said to them, 'Shall I cru-

cify your King?' The chief priests answered,
'We have no king but Caesar.'

"Then he bonded him over to them to be
crucified."

"We have no king but Caesar!" How sadly
true of the time of Jesus! How sadly true today!

Many writers and teachers emphasize the
concept that the Bible is really what might be
called spiritual history, the journey that man
takes from sense to soul. "Through many stories
it tells one story, through many persons it tells
of one person, through history and poetry and
allegory and symbolism it speaks the language
of body, soul, and spirit to record the wander-
ings, the trials and overcomings, the defeats and
victories of us all in this strange journey underneath the stars. All the actors in the drama are
one actor—man—and all places are places that
have been or shall be in your mind and heart.
Remember this, and though sometimes you may
feel lost as indeed most of us have felt in life
itself, you shall find your way from confusion
to understanding.

"The story of the Bible begins with God
and ends with His manifestation in ideal human
expression, which is the Christ of God; and all
in between is told the story of the incarnation
of the sons of heaven upon the earth, with its
clay clinging to their feet and thought, and its

stamp upon their life. Subject to all things, weighed upon by all, they had yet been endowed with that divine spark, breathed into them by the breath of God, which should fulfill the promise of their earthly beginnings. Onward, upward, through births and lives and deaths innumerable the sons of heaven have come, until they should have fulfilled that which was God-planned from the beginning—to know themselves for what they were and are, to become lords and rulers, humbly with God in heaven."

Before the Christ becomes enshrined in his consciousness as lord and ruler of his being, man is drawn to many lesser kings: Moses, Saul, David, Herod, Nero, Caesar.

The populace of Jerusalem acclaimed "no king but Caesar." To the populace of various countries, cities, individuals, who might we say is king today? Individuals as kings are growing ever fewer in number, but there is always some idea, some concept, that is king in our consciousness—and personalities are the embodiment of ideas to us.

What theme is dominant in your consciousness today? Would it be success, or freedom, or security, or physical prowess, or sense-gratification, or power, or authority? What did Caesar represent to the people who acclaimed him that day, and rejected Christ? Whom would we re-

ject, and whom acclaim, if a choice was forced
upon us? Whom do we reject and whom acclaim in our inmost, perhaps unrealized, thought
and heart today?

*I have known many kings, O Christ, and
they have held sway in my mind and heart and
life. Pride has ruled me, and Will, and Zeal,
and Moods, and Intellect. From them all, stern
masters though they be, I have learned and
grown, I pray; until I have come to know that
they were meant to serve me, not I them. And
now I seek to have You, O Lord, rule in my
mind, my heart, my soul, until I come to know
You as my own true self, free, untrammeled, in
command.*

Beyond the Dark Hours

"AND as they led him away, they seized one Simon, of Cyrene, who was coming in from the country, and laid on him the cross, to carry it behind Jesus. And there followed him a great multitude of the people, and of women who bewailed and lamented him. But Jesus turning to them said, 'Daughters of Jerusalem, do not weep for me, but weep for yourselves and for your children. For behold, the days are coming when they will say, "Blessed are the barren, and the wombs that never bore, and the breasts that never gave suck!" Then they will begin to say to the mountains, "Fall on us"; and to the hills, "Cover us." For if they do this when the wood is green, what will happen when it is dry?' "

Judas, an emblem of worldly desire, and Jesus, embodiment of practical idealism, both died in ignominy: Judas by his own hand, Jesus at the hands of the Romans. But the dark hours of Jesus' travail have been dissolved in the bright glory of the Christ, while the dark hours of Judas and of others who conspired for His destruction seem ever darker through the ages; a darkness which can be mitigated only by their atonement, perhaps through many life experiences and by prayer and self-abnegation.

A heavier burden then for the crucifiers than for the Crucified; for to Jesus, going the way of the Cross was not loss but gain.

He chose the way of the Cross to give forever to the world His message of the divine potential in every man, and of man's ultimate victory even over somatic death itself. It is well that, with all compassion for the tragic suffering that Jesus underwent, we can see those dark hours in their true perspective. Viewed alone their darkness assumes a magnitude out of proportion to their true significance. Spiritually they depict the final and complete crossing out of the selfish human self that demands its own way, the radiance and triumph of the victorious

Christ nature that is the ultimate destiny of redeemed humanity.

"Do not weep for me, but weep for yourselves, and for your children," then has a special significance. The ultimate of right attitudes and actions must be good. The ultimate of wrong-doing must be correction (which we often view as punishment). The old Mosaic law that the sins of the parents shall be visited upon the children is not abrogated. It can only be fulfilled by a higher law whose action we invoke by rising to a higher level of responsiveness to life.

"If they do this when the wood is green, what will happen when it is in the dry?" has two implications. The green wood or tree is a symbol of innocence, the dry wood of guilt. Thus, "If the Romans do this to me whom they know to be innocent, what will they do to you and your children whom they will regard as rebellious and guilty?" and also, "If the people can be so guilty in crucifying me, to what further lengths of evil will they proceed?"

In our individual present-day problems, despite our knowledge of the overall law of justice, sometimes we feel that we suffer unjustly. If we can honestly feel that this is so, at least we have the small comfort of thinking we do not really deserve our troubles. But if we know we have "asked for" the difficulties we are in, there is only one recourse we may have: to learn from them and to invoke the forgiveness that Jesus taught us both to grant and to accept.

If in my own ongoing, O Christ, I experience dark hours of my own, whether they be the result of my willingness to espouse a cause and make a sacrifice, or whether they be the result of mistakes I have made, I pray that I shall not be so overcome with self-pity, fear, or sorrow that I shall fail to be steadfast in my faith in resurrection. I shall seek to remember in any time of challenge, "This too shall pass," that weeping may endure for a night, but joy comes with the morning. Lord, I await the dawn.

The Seamless
Robe

"WHEN the soldiers had crucified Jesus they took his garments and made four parts, one for each soldier a part; also his tunic. But the tunic was without seam, woven from top to bottom; So they said to one another, 'Let us not tear it, but cast lots for it to see whose it shall be.' This was to fulfill the scripture. 'They parted my garments among them, and for my clothing they cast lots.' So the soldiers did this."

All four of the Gospels refer to this callous episode. Matthew and John both see it as fulfilling a passage in the Psalms, "They divide my garments among them, and for my raiment they cast lots. John describes it in greatest detail, as we would expect.

The Gospel attributed to John is the most mystical of the four accounts of Jesus' life and ministry. It is the work of a highly inspired mystic, and according to Dummelow "he sits down to write, not a biography, but an interpretation of the life of Christ, and since his method is that of allegory, we are justified in seeking a mystical meaning not only in every saying and every incident, but even in minute details which at first sight seem trivial."

The seamless robe was a beautiful and valuable garment, often taken to be a sign of affluence, sometimes testimony of one of the best kinds of affluence—someone's love, for such garments were often the handiwork of a wife, a mother, a devoted friend, in tribute to the wearer.

Mystically, the seamless robe represents the human body, man's cloak of visibility, by which he has contact with this plane of life. By reason of this seamless robe, he has opportunity to make practical, to prove, to demonstrate, his ability to use the inherent powers and capabilities that God has given him. For this plane is the school of life, in which we are to learn and grow; find some of the blessings this world has to give, and—we pray—some of the blessings that it alone cannot give.

The story of Joseph with his coat of many colors going from his home (heaven) "down" into Egypt (the material world) hints at this. So does the story of the prodigal son, who demanded his inheritance of his father and went into a far country, where he spent his substance in riotous living, and was reduced to menial tasks. When he "came to himself" he said, "I will arise and go to my father." His father saw him coming and had a new robe prepared for him.

Charles Fillmore indicates that the seamless robe represents the body of our regeneration, "a consciousness of the indestructible unity of life and substance in the body consciousness."

Henry VanDyke, in his beautiful poem "A Legend of Service," refers to
"a seamless robe for Truth's great bridal meet
And needing but one thread to be complete."

Lord, I would make my body a seamless robe for Truth's great bridal meet. No longer will I denigrate my body or its functions. I discern it to be spiritual in essence. I bless it as the robe of spirit. I rejoice in its beauty and its wondrous construction. I do not bow down to it to serve it or worship it, but seek to redeem it from any tendency to impute to it desires that are unworthy, since these, if they exist, have their origin not in the body but in the sensual desires of the personal consciousness of the indweller. I praise and give thanks for all my body has done, is doing, and will do for me, as I better understand its true nature.

Father, Forgive
Them

"AND when they came to the place which is called The Skull, there they crucified him, and the criminals, one on the right and one on the left. And Jesus said, 'Father, forgive them; for they know not what they do.' And they cast lots to divide his garments."

It was the darkest hour in human history, and the gentlest and most loving of men was being crucified on Calvary's hill.

Perhaps you have been to Jerusalem. Even though the city has been many times destroyed and built again since Jesus' time, many of the landmarks appear to be very much as they must

have been then. You may stroll through the
Old City, and if so, possibly beyond one of the
ancient walls, where you will see a sign arched
over the entry to a kind of a lane: "The Garden
Tomb." You turn into the lane and are approaching an informal garden. There are olive
trees, and winding walks bordered by a tangle
of garden flowers. You come to some steps and
descend to an ancient pavement, and a tomb
which some people believe to have been the
final resting place for Jesus' body after His
crucifixion. As you face the tomb and look upward to a steep, almost vertical embankment
of earth and rock, you see in it the huge, crude
likeness of a skull. Above it is what appears to
be an almost level area, now used as a Moslem
cemetery. It is on this slightly sloping hill that
the crucifixion is believed to have taken place,
at Golgotha, "a place of a skull."

There from the lips of Jesus, fastened to the
rood, His hands and feet pierced by the cruel
nails, come the words, "Father, forgive them;
for they know not what they do." This is the
first of the so-called seven last words spoken
from the cross.

We are punished not for our sins, but by
them, it has been said. On this basis what sorrows must have been invited by those who cried
for Jesus' blood, for those who made the cross,

for those who drove the nails! Events have long, long shadows . . . shadows that even the elements on that day are said to have reflected. For from the restless sea there rose a murky haze that darkened the sun, and cast an ominous pall upon the morbid throng.

Well might the all-wise Jesus pray for their forgiveness. His anguish, however deep, was for but a few hours, its shadows to be dispelled in lasting light. The darkness of His persecutors must surely long have laid a heavy burden on their souls. Jesus knew the law. He had voiced it to them time and again: "With the judgment you pronounce you will be judged," and "all who take the sword will perish by the sword."

I forgive all men their transgressions. I forgive myself. I let the finger of denial erase every sin or "falling short" that I have charged to myself. I say to the part of my being that is likely to fall short, "Thy sins are forgiven." "Sin no more, lest a worse thing befall thee." I deny in thought the tendency to err, and hold myself firmly to the Christ Spirit, which is my divine self, my sinless impulse and power. (Adapted from Charles Fillmore.)

The Cross

"ONE of the criminals who were hanged railed at him, saying, 'Are you not the Christ? Save yourself and us!' But the other rebuked him, saying, 'Do you not fear God, since you are under the same sentence of condemnation? And we indeed justly; for we are receiving the due reward of our deeds; but this man has done nothing wrong.'

"And he said, 'Jesus, remember me when you come in your kingly power.' And he said to him, 'Truly, I say to you, today you will be with me in Paradise.' "

The Cross represents the seemingly divergent forces of life: the opposites, spirit and matter, positive and negative, good and bad, represented as divided by the horizontal arm of the cross—unified by the vertical, which cancels out apparent separation and makes them one.

It symbolizes the very body of man, standing erect with arms outstretched, risen out of his evolutionary heritage from the lower kingdoms.

Mystically it represents that point in spiritual awareness where man's focus of interest is no longer centered in the body but "crosses over" from the trunk of the body to the head at the "place of a skull."

Jesus used the term symbolically when He said, "If any man would come after me, let him deny himself and take up his cross and follow me." And Paul, alluding to the warring of the two sides of our human nature, writes "that he might create in himself one new man, so making peace, and might reconcile us both to God in one body through the cross, thereby bringing the hostility to an end."

Here we have allusions to the kind of crosses that everyone has to meet in life from time to time: the challenges and problems, the burdens of life that we must uplift and carry, and in doing so call forth at least a portion of the great potential that is in us all.

The preoccupation with symbols that we can apply to our own daily living may often thereby serve a useful purpose. From the Christian story of that darkest Friday one might take Jesus' promise, "Today you will be with me in Paradise," as a promise to all of us, reminding us that "now is the acceptable time; behold, now is the day of salvation," even though we seem to be "crucified" between two thieves, the past and the future that would rob us of a full realization of present possibilities.

But preeminently the Cross becomes the symbol of travail and triumph of the Son of God; of Jesus, crucified between two less worthy men in the most torturous and cruel death that sadistic man could inflict upon a man, a fate usually restricted to the most depraved and evil criminals. To the taunting of the unrepentant criminal He gave no answer, but to the other, who pled, "Remember me when you come into your kingly power," He responded with the promise already cited (and which Lamsa asserts should read, "I say unto you today, thou shalt be with me in paradise").

Today—with me—in Paradise. No delay in the dear love of God, no "great gulf fixed" between God's greatest Son and one of the least.

Even there on the cross, in the dark hour of pain, the love of Jesus reached out to others, past the confusion of that spontaneous cry of childhood—"Remember me!"—into the calm knowing of His manhood.

Jesus did not see men as other men saw themselves and others. Past their human frailties of selfishness and avarice and cunning, He had beheld a vision of man as God saw him in the beginning, full of grace and truth, having and exercising dominion over his personal world of sense and over the outward world of manifestation. When His impatience and indignation were kindled against men it was because they so misrepresented the true and hidden self of them that He saw and because their ignorance of that finer self caused others grief.

As for Himself, He was not misled. His faith was unfaltering. Let them do what they might, it was passing. Those who sat in darkness should see a great light. The light that He had found, they should find, too. They were fearful, they were cunning, they were cruel, they were ill: and only because they did not see, they did not know, they did not understand. There was a light within them, the light of the Father's indwelling presence. To let that light shine forth was freedom. No darkness could hide that brightness from His sight.

They would not wrong Him if only they understood. He was their friend. Some day men

would call Him the greatest friend man has
ever had. They would love Him as He loved
them. If only they would understand!

And because they would not, they would
tend to one of two extremes, complete indul-
gence of the physical nature, or an attempt to
reject that nature entirely. They would attempt
to cut things so fine that there would be one
side without the other. They would like to eliminate all painful experiences from their life,
claiming a freedom from God's law, rather than
freedom within the law. And perhaps because
the story of Jesus bothered them, or possibly because they could not reconcile it with their ways
of reasoning, they would reduce the whole
drama of Golgotha to a potpourri of symbolism,
even reducing Jesus Himself to a symbolical
character, as if in doing so they strengthened
the claim that if we could only think right, feel
right, speak right, and act right there would be
no more problems, no pain, no shadows. As if,
indeed, we had already reached that "new Jerusalem, down out of heaven from God," and
heard a great voice saying, "God . . . will wipe
away every tear from their eyes, and death shall
be no more, neither shall there be morning nor
crying nor pain, any more for the former things
have passed away."

While we are still in the realm of earth and

time, however, it is difficult successfully to deny that these things still exist, even though we may well assert that they have no ultimate reality.

Everything is real in its own plane; only a shadow of what is real in a higher plane. The Revelator here is describing a level of awareness beyond the mundane world. While we are in this mundane world we are (at least to a degree) subject to its laws. No matter how spiritual we are or believe ourself to be, we must eat and sleep and breathe. We do not eliminate problems by denying their existence, but rather by evoking the abilities that enable us to solve them, and find the blessing that is a part of the solution.

Jesus could have rejected the way of the Cross. He chose instead to face it, and reach past it. Had there been no Crucifixion there would have been no Resurrection.

I claim the blessing in every experience. I cross out or cancel every negation by a positive affirmation. Where I have seen only a cross of affliction, I now see a crown of attainment. I endeavor to see all men as Christ sees them, victorious, triumphant, splendid, claiming and exercising their dominion over themselves and whatever challenges them from within or without. I claim the promise, "You will know the truth, and the truth will make you free."

Jesus Loved Them

"BUT standing by the cross of Jesus were his mother, and his mother's sister, Mary the wife of Clopas, and Mary Magdalene. When Jesus saw his mother, and the disciple whom he loved standing by, he said to his mother, 'Woman, behold, your son!' Then he said to the disciple, 'Behold your mother!' And from that hour the disciple took her to his own home."

In times of worldly success and favor there are many who gather around to acclaim and to share acclaim. In times of seeming adversity there often are few. But at the cross of Jesus

there were two whom He dearly loved, two who
dearly loved Him.

They were Mary, His mother, and John,
the apostle. Whatever the bonds of friendship
that may have linked them until then, the words
of Jesus established a new tie. "Behold, your
mother," He said to John; and to Mary, "Behold, your son!"

The words of Jesus are precious both because of their scarcity and because of their import. Of all His words, perhaps these were most
precious to Mary, for they tell what in His
recorded words at least is not otherwise com-
municated. They tell of His deep love for His
mother. From the beginning of His ministry
Jesus did not see much of His family. Their
meetings seem to have been few and not very
satisfying. More and more Jesus was reaching
out into the world. Away from them? It must
have been frightening and confusing to them.
To the traditional Jewish mind the discourses
of Jesus were little short of heretical. They
menaced His own safety, even His life. Surely,
the thought of all this must have gone through
Mary's mind there, at that lonely Cross. Had
her son misunderstood her anxiety? Had He
grown so tall in spiritual stature as to have
grown away from her? Did He think of her
only in the impersonal way that His question

of long before had implied? She remembered
the words "Who is my mother, and who are my
brothers?"

Here was His answer; warm and tender was
his love of her: "Behold, your son! . . . Behold,
your mother!" Even in the valley of the shadow
His thought was for her. Though He was the
Son of God and Christ of the world, yet too He
was still her son Jesus.

Because I love You much, O God, I find I
love all people more. I had thought I might miss
the things and the people of my world as I
turned from them to You. But in turning to
Your presence I find here those I love who love
me. I come closer to them as I reach inwardly to
You. Being one with You I am close to all that
is. My mind and heart are merged with Yours.
I in them, and You in me, and they in us.

Was Jesus Forsaken?

"**N**OW from the sixth hour there was darkness over all the land until the ninth hour. And about the ninth hour Jesus cried with a loud voice, 'Eli, Eli, lama sabachthani?' that is, 'My God, my God, why hast thou forsaken me?'

Had God forsaken Jesus on the cross? If the Father should desert this holiest of men, what hope then exists for any of us? Were God's assurances of old abrogated in Jesus? "As I was with Moses, so I will be with you; I will not fail you, or forsake you," was His promise to Joshua. And Jesus himself had said to Peter in the garden only the night before, "Do you think that I cannot appeal to my Father, and he will at once send me more than twelve legions of angels? But how then should the scriptures be fulfilled, that it must be so?"

How then could God have forsaken Jesus? He did not.

Neither did Jesus believe that God had forsaken Him. If so, would He have interceded with the Father for the forgiveness of His enemies, or would He have commended His spirit into the Father's hands?

It is said that all men pray in times of dire distress even if they do not consciously pray at other times. Their prayer is not usually the consciously thought-out prayer of the missal, but the spontaneous utterance of whatever, welling up from the subconsciousness, symbolizes prayer to them. Often it reaches back if they have learned in maturity to their childhood impressions and memories.

Men who have not consciously thought of God since childhood except perhaps profanely, will involuntarily address their Maker as they reach the limits of their human resources and face disaster. The grim apothegm, wrung out of the experiences of World War II, "There are no atheists in foxholes," confirms this. Persons of foreign birth who have long since deserted their native tongue for the common

speech of those around them, will find themselves uttering phrases from the long-forgotten
terms of their forbears.

In times of deepest need our heart reaches
past our mind and cries out the simple utterances
of prayer, in which the words may or may not
be significant.

It was so with Jesus. He had reached into a
knowing, conscious faith that was in some respects a far cry from the ancient prayers of His
people. The throng around the cross were familiar with Greek and Hebrew. They could not
understand Him when he cried out, "Eli, Eli,
lama sabachthani!" They thought He was calling upon Elijah to save Him.

He was praying an ancient prayer of His
people, preserved in verse one of the twenty-
second Psalm.

He prayed in Aramaic.

It was the language He had learned as a
boy.

"My God, my God, why hast thou forsaken
me?" is the familiar translation of the words,
but George Lamsa, Syrian scholar whose people
still speak the language and preserve the ancient
customs of Jesus' times, declares that this passage should have been translated, "My God, my
God, for this was I kept!" The word *shbakthani*,
he says, is derived from the word *shbak* which

means to keep, reserve, leave, spare, forgive, allow, permit. The last letter of *shbakthani* indicates first person singular.

His rendition of the wording seems in keeping with Jesus' prayer: "Now is my soul troubled. And what shall I say? 'Father, save me from this hour'? No, for this purpose I have come to this hour."

The ancient rendering speaks to the heart; it is what any of us might cry. The more recent rendering speaks to the mind, and such a mind as Jesus' might well have meant it so, even in the agony of His human travail.

"Sweet is the promise, I will not forget thee.
Nothing can molest or turn my soul away.
E'en though the night be dark within the valley,
Just beyond is shining one eternal day.

"I will not forget thee or leave thee.
In my hands I'll hold thee,
In my arms I'll fold thee.
I will not forget thee or leave thee.
I am thy redeemer, I will care for thee."
　　　　　(Hymn, "I Will Not Forget Thee,"
　　　　　　　　by Charles Gabriel).

"I Thirst"

"AFTER this Jesus, knowing that was now finished, said (to fulfill the scripture), 'I thirst.' A bowl full of vinegar stood there, so they put a sponge full of the vinegar on hyssop, and held it to his mouth."

He had forgiven His enemies.

He had assured the repentant thief that he should find his way into heaven.

He had shown His love and concern for His mother Mary and for John.

He had again announced His divine purpose and its fulfillment.

He revealed again His capacity for sharing the joys and sorrows of humanity, in His cry, wrung out of the body's anguish, "I thirst."

That cry of Jesus speaks of all the woes of men, hungering and thirsting, as often they do not consciously realize, after righteousness.

We become thirsty and we drink, but we become thirsty again. Life is like that. We thirst for some new experience, some new possession. We attain it and (maybe) for a time we are satisfied. But let us not be surprised if we thirst again, and with a greater thirst.

Shall we ignore the world and its attractions, then? Shall we become sophists and pessimists? Shall we avoid the pleasures of life because of possible disappointment?

Dodging a problem does not solve it. To give up trying because in trying we have found the wrong answer does not satisfy us. Nothing will satisfy us but the right answer; for "the gate is narrow, and the way is hard, that leads to life, and those who find it are few."

The greatest of these was sitting by a well one day when a woman of Samaria came to draw water. "Whoever drinks of the water that I shall give him will never thirst," He said.

She was astonished, not only because of His words, but because He, a Jew, should speak to her, a Samaritan: "The water that I shall give

him will become in him a spring of water welling up to eternal life."

What is this water of which the Master
spoke, that not merely allays but satisfies the
thirst? We know that satisfaction does not come
of material things alone, though it includes
them, surely. They are accessories to happiness
and content, but must be accompanied by inward peace to be thoroughly enjoyable. And
how shall we find this? Only by drinking of the
fount of spiritual knowledge.

Truly on that day the body of Jesus knew
thirst for its own need. The soul of Jesus thirsted
not for His own soul's need, but for the souls
of others, that they might know the truth for
which He lived—and lives.

*It is when we are hungry that we seek for
food to appease our hunger, when we are thirsty
that we seek for water to quench our thirst; and
because we do hunger and thirst after righteousness, that we may know Your truth, O God, that
we also know that we shall be filled. We give
thanks for the assurance that You will "lead us
unto living fountains of water," even "a spring
of water welling up to eternal life."*

"It Is Finished!"

"WHEN Jesus had received the vinegar, he said, 'It is finished'; and he bowed his head and gave up his spirit."

All four of the Gospels mention that Jesus cried out, but only John reports His words.

Jesus had brought His message to Palestine prior to the ordeal of trial and crucifixion. With the crucifixion He perpetuated His message in a manner so compelling and dramatic that it was preserved for all time and for all the world to know.

In the tenth chapter of the gospel of John, He says: "I am the good shepherd; and I know my own and my own know me, as the Father knows me and I know the Father; and I lay down my life for the sheep. And I have other sheep, that are not of this fold; I must bring them also, and they will heed my voice. So there shall be one flock, one shepherd. For this reason the Father loves me, because I lay down my life, that I may take it again. No one takes it from me, but I lay it down of my own accord. I have power to lay it down, and I have power to take it again."

What was the end of Jesus' ministry at the time and in the place that it occurred was the beginning of a far greater ministry. For all that He lost, He gained what was infinitely greater. It is so for those who follow Him.

We may take the measure of small events and small people closely. Perspective is required for the true measure of a great event, a great subject, a great person.

In Jesus' time few if any understood Him.

In our present day, misconceptions still exist. We can only see in Him, in His purpose, in His fulfilling of it, what we are prepared to see.

In our own evaluation of Him, we reveal our own relative stature. We involuntarily estimate His vision in terms of our own sight, or insight.

He has been called poor because He had few

possessions ("the Son of man has nowhere to lay his head"), yet He wore the "tunic . . . without seam" (actually a mystic allusion to His glorious body); He fed thousands of people who came, apparently beyond their mealtimes, to hear Him: He stilled the waves of the sea at His word, commanded the deaf to hear, the blind to see, the demoniac to let go his demon —even the dead to rise again, as in the case of His friend Lazarus, in what seemed like a prefigure of His own resurrection.

He has been called "despised," "reckoned among the transgressors," yet the wise men heralded His birth and hung on the words of His youth, and "the common people" as well as others "heard him gladly," and the calendars of most of the modern world date events with relation to the conjectured time of His birth.

He has been called a myth, yet no one who has ever lived before or since has so captured the imagination or so won the hearts of men, or inspired men to such mighty deeds as He.

He has been called "a man of sorrows, and acquainted with grief," yet His life and His teachings were a gospel of joyous fulfillment, and His wit is only surpassed by His wisdom. Long recognized as the greatest of spiritual and moral teachers, He is coming to be recognized as a great psychologist as well. What were considered to be miracles in His own time are so often becoming recognized as applied science, that we tend to look for a hidden law expressed in the things He did which still baffle our understanding.

Long considered to be an impractical idealist, the expounder of doctrines inimical to the businessman and dangerous to government, now scarcely an orator or a statesman but quotes His words to lend weight and authority to their own. He might have marshalled armies and used bloodshed and death to make Himself king of Judaea in the days of Caesar and Pilate. The bloodless triumph of ideas has made Him the uncrowned king of kings.

"There are also many other things which Jesus did;" says John, "were every one of them to be written, I suppose that the world itself could not contain the books that would be written."

In my thought of myself, O loving Presence, I may see myself as in a mirror darkly, as Paul did; but I know that in Your sight and therefore in the ultimate truth of my being, I am not limited by what I see in the mirror. With Your help I envision myself as I am in spirit, victorious, triumphant, splendid. I dwell in the consciousness that all that I am yet to be is already established in the heavenly vision. It is finished, as the pattern of the oak tree is contained in the acorn, as the pattern of the rose in the plant of which it is the flower. In time, in space, in form this is a progressive process. In spirit, it is complete and perfect now.

Into Thy Hands

"THEN Jesus, crying with a loud voice, said, 'Father, into thy hands I commit my spirit!' and having said this, he breathed his last."

Only Luke records this final utterance of Jesus, the "seventh word" from the cross.

If for a moment in the humanly felt agony of the cross, Jesus actually did cry out that God had forsaken Him, these final words erase them, and should, forever from the acceptance of mankind. And this to our comfort and reassurance, for if indeed God forsook Jesus in His greatest hour of need, what hope would there be for the rest of us?

195

The words of the old familiar hymn echo again in our thought, "I will not forget thee or leave thee . . . I will care for thee."

In the seven last words of Jesus on the cross are depicted His supreme renunciation, the fulfillment of His own triumph over Himself and His temporal ministry that should make Him the Savior of the world. They become a kind of outline of the challenges and overcomings that (on a lesser scale) we all have to make. In this, the seventh word might well be taken as a starting point for us: "Into thy hands I commit my spirit."

This is the *alpha* and *omega* of meditation and prayer, the proper beginning, the inevitable ending. For what is prayer but the turning to the presence of God as a very present help and resource? What is prayer but a pouring out of our heart's longing and our human need? And when this has been done, and instead of talking to Him, we listen for His response, what shall the last word be but "Into thy hands I commit my spirit"?

We journey out into the far country of this mundane world, a yielding of ourself in His name to the initiation of mundane experience. We grow, we learn, we rejoice, we mourn, we fear and find faith, and supplant faith by greater faith, until faith becomes manifest in works, and our human sense of separation from Him and from one another is displaced by the sense of at-one-ment (which is what atonement really means). We find that even in this mundane world we are not far from the kingdom. And so we come the full round from hopeful faith to faith fulfilled, and what was at first almost a plea becomes a paean of rejoicing, "Father, into thy hands I commit my spirit."

I am now in the presence of pure Being, and immersed in the Holy Spirit of life, love, and wisdom.

I acknowledge Thy presence and Thy power, O blessed Spirit; in Thy divine wisdom I now erase my mortal limitations and from Thy pure substance of love bring into manifestation my world, according to Thy perfect law.

The Veil of the Temple

"AND Jesus cried again with a loud voice and yielded up his Spirit. And behold, the curtain of the temple was torn in two, from top to bottom; and the earth shook, and the rocks were split."

Clouds and storms and tremblings are always associated with human sorrows and tragedies and dramas. There were "thunderings and lightnings, and a thick cloud upon the mountain, and a very loud blast," when Moses received the Ten Commandments.

Elijah, fleeing from the wrath of Jezebel, and brooding over the backsliding of the Israelites, climbed up Mount Horeb, and "a great and strong wind rent the mountains, and broke in pieces the rocks . . . and after the wind an earthquake . . . and after the earthquake a fire." After the fire, a still small voice gave Elijah his inspiration.

Whether the elements reflected the moods of the persons, or were actually the inner upheavals of human motion is never very clear.

It was not very clear in the time of Moses or Elijah. It was not very clear in the time of Jesus' crucifixion, for we read that "from the sixth hour," which would be noon, until "the ninth hour," which would be midafternoon, "there was darkness over all the land." And the curtain of the temple was torn in two, from top to bottom; and the earth shook, and the rocks were split;" and to such an extent that "the tombs also were opened, and many bodies of the saints who had fallen asleep were raised, and coming out of the tombs after his resurrection they went into the holy city and appeared to many."

Looking back on an event which has moved us very deeply emotionally, it is very difficult to dissociate the subjective from the objective. The way we picture things now is in terms of the way we *felt* them. It is not to disparage the narrators, notably Matthew, to say that he seems to have been overcome when describing these momentous events, and that he may have imputed to nature some of the reactions that were in the minds and hearts of himself and others.

The rending of garments is a Hebraic cymbol of mourning. Job, in his affliction, rent his mantle; David rent his clothes in his grief over the death of Jonathan and Saul, and for the house of Israel. Joel, exhorting the children of Zion to repentance, admonishes them: "Rend your hearts and not your garments."

Matthew may have intended a purely symbolical rather than a literal meaning to the rending of the curtain of the temple, signifying that the barrier between heaven and earth, between God and man, was abolished through the death of Jesus and His subsequent resurrection.

Jesus yielding up his Spirit, or as it is often referred to, "giving up the ghost," though taken to signify His death, has another more mystical meaning. At the beginning of His ministry, when He was baptized by John, Luke describes this (3:22), "And the Holy Spirit descended upon him in bodily form, as a dove, and a voice came from heaven, 'Thou art my beloved Son; with thee I am well pleased." This was Jesus' divine commission.

On the cross Jesus completed the mission that He accepted at the time of His baptism. In yielding up the spirit (the Holy Spirit), He is saying to God in effect: "I have accomplished what you gave me to do. It is finished. Into your hands I commit my spirit."

The veil of partition in my own consciousness that would separate earth and heaven, man and God, is rent. I too have a commission, that of becoming in fact what I am in Truth, a son of God, endued with infinite possibilities, coming step by step into greater awareness of oneness of my own powers and facilities, my oneness with God, oneness with my fellow men, and with all creation.

At the Foot of the
Cross

"WHEN the centurion and those who were with him, keeping watch over Jesus, saw the earthquake and what took place, they were filled with awe and said, 'Truly this was the Son of God!'

"There were also many women there, looking on from afar, who had followed Jesus from Galilee, ministering to him; among them were Mary Magdalene, and Mary the mother of James and Joseph, and the mother of the sons of Zebedee."

"You must be a Christian!" is something any follower of the Way would be delighted to have someone say of him. But in the early years following the time of Jesus the term was a taunt hurled at the faithful by nonbelievers. "In Antioch the disciples were for the first time called Christians."

Today thousands of churches surmount their steeples or adorn their walls or altar tables with crosses as the paramount emblem of their faith; and millions wear items of jewelry adorned with the sign of the cross.

On that day that Jesus offered up His life at Golgotha heavy clouds hid the sun, the very earth seemed to tremble, and many construed these as signs of God's displeasure, as well as an outpicturing of their own feelings of sorrow and foreboding. None, perhaps not even Jesus Himself, would have imagined that the Cross which was the scene of His suffering would ever become the symbol of men's faith in Him.

On either side of Him, the criminals, one of them crying, "Are you not the Christ? Save yourself and us!" Along the highway, the vulgar, the curious, reviling Him, "wagging their heads, and saying, 'you who would destroy the temple and build it in three days, save yourself! If you are the Son of God, come down from the cross!' "

At the foot of the cross were soldiers casting lots for His garments.

There too were the chief priests, with the scribes and elders, mocking Him: "He saved others; he cannot save himself."

There too were John, the beloved disciple, and Mary His mother, whom John was to take with him to his own home from that very hour. With them were two other Marys, one the wife of Clopas, the other the Magdalene; Salome, mother of Zebedee's children, Joanna; and a little farther off, many who had followed Jesus from Galilee into Jerusalem at the beginning of the week that was to change their world, and worlds to come.

The curious, the mockers, the morbid, the fearful, the prayerful. What did they think? How did they feel? What did they see as they looked upon the Cross? It remained for the Greek centurion to exclaim, "Truly this was the Son of God!"

It was nearly sundown when Joseph of Arimathaea and Nicodemus arrived, and gently removed the body of Jesus from the cross. Joseph had gone secretly to Pilate and obtained permission to care for His body. Nicodemus brought myrrh and aloes and linen cloths with which to anoint and clothe the body, and they laid Him in a new sepulchre in a garden close by, and placed before the door of the tomb a great stone.

And it was dark.

Had I been present on that fateful day, with which members of the throng could I be identified? Where am I now in thought of Him, and of that in me which is most like Him? Do I crucify Him? Do I glorify Him? Do I truly love and serve Him? "As you did it to one of the least of these my brethren, you did it to me," He said. So I seek to think and feel and say and do that which is approved by His nature within me: and if I serve not greatly, it shall at least be gratefully, In His name and spirit.

Before the Dawn

"NEXT day, that is, the day of Preparation, the chief priests and the Pharisees gathered before Pilate and said, 'Sir, we remember how that impostor said, while he was still alive, "After three days I will rise again." Therefore order the sepulchre to be made secure until the third day, lest his disciples go and steal him away, and tell the people, "He has risen from the dead," and the last fraud will be worse than the first.'

"Pilate said to them, 'You have a guard of

soldiers; go, make it as secure as you can.' So they went and made the sepulchre secure by sealing the stone and setting a guard."

Friday was called the day of Preparation. Saturday was the Sabbath. In the progress from Palm Sunday to Easter Sunday, Saturday was the time of waiting, the time that is always darkest just before the dawn.

Pilate seemed to remember what even those closest to Jesus did not take as literally as he, "After three days I will rise again." There is a perverse streak in human nature (sadly typified by Pilate) that finds it easier to believe the worst than the best; easier to enlarge upon the negative than upon the positive. An illustration that seems trivial because it is so common has almost lost significance for us, is revealing. Ask a person how he feels. If he feels good, he will respond with a word or two: "Okay," or "Fine," or "I'm all right." But if he isn't feeling well, he tends to expound upon symptoms at length.

Pilate feared the fulfillment of Jesus' declaration. The disciples and other followers of Jesus found His words, as we say, "too good to be true." Even the women who were at the foot of the cross with palliatives to ease His pain, and at the dawning of Sunday morning brought ointment and spices to anoint and embalm His body, were terrified by the thought of its being stolen. They did not expect it to be risen.

We pray and believe not what we say. We ask and are surprised that there is an answer, as sometimes we may well be, for we are likely to receive from life not what we ask for but what we expect.

In most of the major projects of our life, there is a time of preparation, a time of waiting, and finally a time of fulfillment. Of these the time of waiting requires the greatest faith, the greatest steadfastness, the greatest patience.
"There is a tide in the affairs of men,

Which, taken at the flood, leads on to fortune," the poet says. Those of faint heart may give way to despair; those of stout heart await the turning of the tide.

I believe in good outcomes. I expect the good. I await its fulfillment. I let patience have her perfect work. I work as I wait; work as if everything depends on me, and pray as if everything depends on God. As the nature of God in Jesus was mighty to overcome even the "last enemy," so I know Him to be mighty in me to perfect and fulfill that which concerns me and those I love. In quietness and in confidence I find my fulfillment.